A gift has been made by:

Jan Gooch

In honor of

CALS

wild
sugar
DESSERTS

wild sugar DESSERTS

SKYE CRAIG AND LYNDEL MILLER

NEW HOLLAND

For my sister Erin for a lifetime of love and inspiration in twenty-six short years.

For my father, Barry 'Boots' Seymour, who raised me as his own, who taught me to embrace life and all those in it, to love and respect, to play, always find room for humour, and to greet every day anew.

THIS BOOK BELONGS TO:

_____

WHO *loves*
IT MORE THAN
chocolate

Acknowledgements

Hugs and Kisses

From Skye

What a wonderfully juicy journey creating this book has been. *Wild Sugar Desserts* has only come about because of the wonderful talents of so many people who have given up much of their time.

First and foremost, to one of the most creative and juicy people I have ever met, Lyndel Miller. I feel incredibly blessed to have created this book with you, my friend. You are truly gifted in so many ways. Thank you for all that you are.

Thank you so very much Mum and Dad for being there tirelessly throughout all Wild Sugar endeavours. I would not be doing this without your love and help. I love you x.

To my sister Erin, who inspired me constantly with her passion for growing fresh produce, Australian native ingredients and our shared insatiable passion for cooking—and even more so, eating! I miss you and I'm keeping it all alive.

To my chef extraordinaire cousin, Kylie Craig, who has nurtured my cooking skills a great deal. I couldn't be more grateful. You are the reason I am writing this book in the first place.

To Maggie Good, Michael Hatchett, Suzanne, Kathy, Mark, Cam, Danny and Christine for all of the beauty, guidance and a shared love of the sweetest things in life.

Pete Turner for cracking coconuts during the early days of Wild Sugar and the mutual love of a good laugh.

Andrew Cottle for introducing me to raw desserts and a healthier way of being—an inspiration to many.

To Karla, Helen and Adele for your lifelong friendships and sharing your beautiful recipes with us.

To Michelle and Dean Jessop, David and Gilda Wise, Michelle Spense, Anthony Nelson, Melanie Starr Ingersol, Jared Ingersol and Rene Foster, for the shared passion for food, friendship and life. You are my family.

To Justine, Melinda and Tracy from Chefs Ink, Celeste, Lliane, Jodi and Fiona from New Holland Publishers thank you for your incredible work, believing in me and making our dreams come true.

To the producers of MasterChef, George, Matt and Gary for allowing me the opportunity to cook with some of the best chefs and for your guidance and help throughout MasterChef Series 2 and beyond. To the MasterChef house co-ordinators Kristine and Mikey Moo—thanks for putting up with us. You are both incredible people and I miss you both. To my dear friends who now feel like family: Alvin for making me laugh 24/7, Adele for your heart, Claire for your beauty and grace, Courtney for your cake, Sharnee and Pete for the giggles, Marion for the inspiration and friendship, Jonno and Devon for the entertainment, Jimmi for the curries and Pete for taking us for rides on the bike. Joining forces with you fellow foodies is simply a blessing.

To family and friends all over the world, you inspire me endlessly and I am blessed to have you in my life.

From Lyndel

As a mother of two small children, creating this book means that I have had a lot of help along the way.

Firstly, to my colleague and dear friend Skye Craig, thank you for giving me this opportunity. It is such a gift to share all that I am and all that I love. I am eternally grateful. You will always have a special place in my heart. I feel privileged to know you and your family. It has been an amazing experience. I will treasure it all my fellow gypsy. Love always.

To my Mum, Carole Seymour, who made me the person I am, thank you for sharing your love of food with me, you are my culinary hero. I love you more than words can say.

To my sister, Victoria Sichler, and to Kirsten Baker, thank you to the both of you, the people in my life who offer the support and truth, I couldn't do without you. You are the best friends anyone could possibly want or need.

To my sister, Sarah Seymour, kisses of appreciation for championing me from the beginning, the inspiration pages and valued feedback. I love you.

My brother David Sichler for loving music as much as I do. Thanks for the tunes, you rock!

Georgia, for just being the incredible teacher you are! You give me strength.

To my other wonderful family, Barrie, Isla, Amanda, Roy, Katie, James, Beau and Jake. I am grateful to have you in my life.

To all my recipe testers and my recipe tasters, especially Beau and Jake Maynard for never refusing an invitation. Thank you for your time, effort and investment in me.

To my inspirational BFF Chemai McKendry who, despite the demands of mothering and home-schooling seven (yes seven!), still found time for me. You are incredible and I miss you.

To all my family and beautiful friends, all of who have shared many a meal at my table over the years, and have encouraged my artistic and culinary enthusiasm and explorations, been kind even when I have failed miserably, laughed with me, danced with me and left me feeling always that going the extra mile for those you love is always worth the effort. You give me the reason to want to celebrate and share.

And last but not least, to my husband Simon, the love of my life, who knowing how much this meant to me, happily re-arranged our life to make it happen. I love you with all my heart. I couldn't have done this without you. My darling children, Tahlia and Sam, the greatest treasures in my life, I love you, you inspire me daily. You can have the computer back now, Mum is off to the gym!

Contents

Introduction

We love sweeties.
We love eating them.
We love making them.
We love sharing them.

But what we love the most is the beautiful relationship that exists between sweets and life's varied experiences.

Like most kids, following mum around the kitchen as she cooked and licking the bowl afterwards was our first motivation for cooking. So much to intrigue us—the new smells, tastes and textures. But really, we just loved to fill our bellies with all the goodness of mother's love. Our feelings about life and love are inextricably linked to creating and enjoying desserts...the best part of any meal.

Although simple, sweets can be the very thing that brings us together in complete delight, whether for celebration or for comfort. Sweets are a universal language and they carry you through life's journey.

Between us, we have lived in faraway places and immersed ourselves in the design, art and music industries, but at the end of the day, what is most important to us is family, food and friends. This book is the essence of who we are. It is a culmination of our gypsy wanderings.

Wild Sugar Desserts is a celebration of the emotional connection so many of us have with sweets, which is influenced by circumstance, emotions, family, history and the company you share.

We don't claim to be three Michelin-star chefs nor Country Woman's Association baking betties. We're simply home cooks, wildly passionate about nurturing others with our desserts.

United by our affection for sweets and gorgeous local produce, we have laughed, cried and danced our way through writing this book. *Wild Sugar Desserts* took us on a trip down memory lane and made us smile widely. We hope to share some inspiration.

Two crazy ladies, one book of sweets.

Wild sugar desserts—this is cooking with love.

Skye's recipes are marked with this purple symbol.

Lyndel's recipes are marked with this pink symbol.

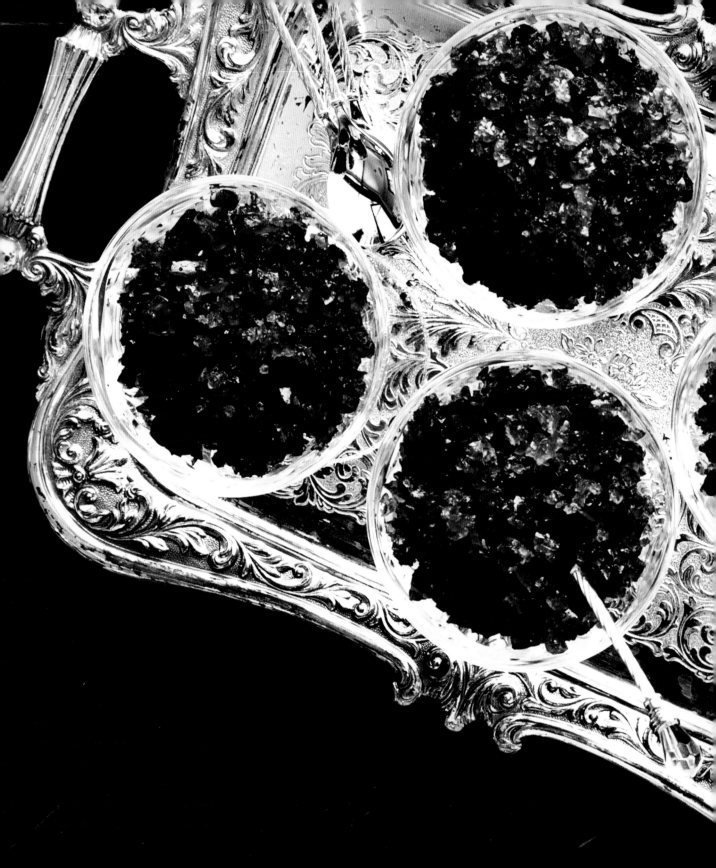

Building Blocks

Have fun playing with these building blocks. They are your basics and essentials for building something spectacular.

Quick Toffee

Cooking time: 20 minutes

You can leave the toffee plain or sprinkle with a flavouring of your choice.

1 cup (220g/7oz) caster (superfine) sugar

FLAVOURS
Cinnamon: 1 teaspoon ground cinnamon
Ginger: 1 teaspoon ground ginger powder
Dried rose petals and dried berries (I like goji berries)

Place a sheet of baking paper in a baking tray and set aside. Place half of the sugar in a medium to large frypan and heat over a medium heat. When you see the sugar start to melt, stir, starting mostly on the outside of the frypan, ensuring the sugar on the outside of the pan doesn't burn. When you see the sugar starting to melt in the middle of the frypan, start stirring this part too.

Add the other half of the sugar and watch very carefully—no running off to answer the phone, my friends. Once the sugar melts, stir it to ensure that all the sugar crystals have dissolved. When the toffee is a lovely caramel colour, pull off the stove immediately.

Pour onto the baking paper in the tray, making sure that the toffee isn't too thick. If using a flavouring, sprinkle on now. Leave to cool and set. When completely cooled, break the toffee into shards.

Sugar Syrup

Choose to suit your needs.

Note: *If making a dessert which requires a little tang, add in some lemon juice.*

SUGAR SYRUP 450ML (15½FL OZ)

250g (9oz) caster (superfine) sugar

250ml (9fl oz) water

SUGAR SYRUP 375ML (13FL OZ)

200g (7oz) caster (superfine) sugar

200ml (7fl oz) water

SUGAR SYRUP 225ML (8FL OZ)

150g (5oz) caster (superfine) sugar

150ml (5fl oz) water

SUGAR SYRUP 150ML (5FL OZ)

100g (3½oz) caster (superfine) sugar

100ml (3½fl oz) water

In a small or medium saucepan (depending on amount of syrup you are making), combine sugar and water over medium heat, bring to boil. Boil until sugar dissolves, remove from heat and then allow to cool. Store in an airtight container.

Easy Crème Fraîche Ice Cream

Serves 6

Preparation/cooking time: 15 minutes

Freeze: 3 hours for best texture or overnight and into the food processor if you want to make well ahead of time.

I love the simplicity of this recipe. There is no need to pull out a thermometer, make a custard, no frenzied stirring and no big mess to clean up. I have added some yoghurt to the crème fraîche as I just love that slightly tart hit you get right on the roof of your mouth. This makes the most wonderful accompaniment to most desserts. It often balances something sweet with a good hit of that great crème fraîche and yoghurty tang—the perfect partner to a hot and sassy dessert.

200g (7oz) crème fraîche (or sour cream for a cheaper option)

100g (3½oz) plain, unsweetened yoghurt

2 egg whites

50g (1¾oz) caster (superfine) sugar

Beat egg whites to soft peaks, sprinkle the sugar over the top and beat to firm peaks. Fold in the crème fraîche and yoghurt. Place in an airtight container and freeze for around 3 hours, at this point the texture will be creamy and smooth and it is best eaten at this time.

If you want to make well ahead of time, you can freeze completely and then throw your crème fraîche ice cream into a food processor, blend until smooth and serve. Beware, this ice cream will coerce you to eat it endlessly.

Sweet Shortcrust Pastry

You must follow this gorgeous recipe completely for it to work. It is wetter than most sweet shortcrusts when rolling out, so it is important to use the wax paper both underneath and on top. A beautiful, light, buttery pastry that you will long for.

Note: *If your tart base is a little soft, simply remove from oven and take pastry weights out, then bake for another 5 minutes or until pastry is a light gold in colour.*

150g (5oz) unsalted butter, cold, cubed

300g (10½oz) plain (all-purpose) flour

1½ egg yolks

1½ tablespoons (30g/1oz) icing (confectioners') sugar

In a large mixing bowl, rub butter and flour together until well combined and crumbly. In another bowl, combine 3 tablespoons cold water and egg yolk, lightly beat. Then beat in sugar. Add the egg mixture gradually to flour mixture until the dough is well combined. Do not over-work it, take your time, you will get better results this way.

Roll the pastry into a ball, cover with plastic wrap and refrigerate for 30 minutes. Preheat oven to 180°C (350°F/Gas Mark 4).

Lay out sheet of baking paper on kitchen bench, remove plastic wrap and place another sheet of baking paper over the pastry and roll pastry until it is about 5mm (¼in) thick. Now drape pastry over a 28cm (11in) tart tin with removable base, pressing gently into base and sides, trimming where necessary. Prick the pastry all over with a fork.

Freeze pastry for 2 minutes. Pull out of freezer and blind bake by placing some baking paper over the tart case and filling with dried beans, uncooked rice, coins or pastry weights to weigh down pastry so that it will not rise.

To blind bake, place a circle of baking paper, about 5cm (1in) larger than the base of the tart tin, over the pastry and fill with dried beans, uncooked rice, coins (or pennies, if any are still around) to weigh down the pastry so it will not rise.

Maggie Beer's Sour Cream Pastry

There's no doubt about it, Maggie Beer's Sour Cream Pastry is a sure winner. It's lovely and buttery, while forgiving and easy to make. Thank you Maggie for your incredible pastry goodness.

Note: *Put your flour and food processor container in the freezer well ahead of time to make sure that you keep your pastry as cold as possible. Pastry loves the cold. You can also fill a bowl with ice and water to dip your hands in, to keep them cold, but dry them when handling the pastry. Make sure you don't overwork the pastry. For the softest and most delicate pastry, work quickly, as the dough becomes quite fragile as it heats up. Handle it as carefully as you would a baby.*

200g (7oz) chilled, unsalted butter, chopped in small pieces

250g (9oz) plain (all-purpose) flour

2 tablespoons (20g/⅔oz) icing (confectioners') sugar

½ cup (125g/4oz) sour cream

To make pastry, put butter, flour and icing sugar into a food processor, then pulse until the mixture looks like breadcrumbs. Add the sour cream and pulse again until the dough just forms a ball. Be very careful not to over-process. Wrap the dough in plastic wrap and place in the refrigerator for 15 to 20 minutes.

Lightly dust your bench with flour. Remove plastic wrap from dough and roll out until it is 3mm (¼in) thick and line your deep quiche dish or 20cm (8in) tart tin with removable base; no need to butter your dish or tin. Use a fork to prick the pastry all over to remove any air pockets. Place pastry-lined tin in the fridge and chill for 20 minutes.

To blind bake, preheat oven to 200°C (400°F/Gas Mark 6). Line your pastry case with baking paper then cover with pastry weights or rice. Blind bake for 15 minutes, then remove baking paper and pastry weights and bake for another 5 minutes.

Simple Chocolate Ganache

Use this chocolate ganache sauce over ice cream, in Elvis Presley Parfait (see Index), in a tart or in the bottom of a Cinnamon Chocolate Souffle (see Index). You can also use this for icing on a cake. Use a little less cream and add a tablespoon of butter—it will make it gorgeous and glossy. This is truly decadent in its simplicity.

Note: *You can use all dark chocolate or all milk chocolate—whatever tickles your fancy.*

50g (1¾oz) dark (semisweet) chocolate (I like
    Lindt 70% cocoa)

50g (1¾oz) milk chocolate
½ cup pouring cream

Place the chocolate in food processor or chop up into small pieces.

Place the cream in a small saucepan over a medium heat. As soon as you see it start to boil, take it off the heat. Pour the hot cream over the chocolate and stir until smooth and glossy.

Berry Coulis

Serves 4
Preparation time: 15–20 minutes

If you have ever wondered what 'coulis' means, it is French for 'a thin puree'. Make this with your singular choice of berries, or a combination of whatever suits your fancy. Best choices are strawberries, raspberries and blackberries. You can use it as a decorative finish to plated dishes or as an ingredient in mousses, ice creams, sorbets, smoothies or cocktails. I love to put a teaspoon of fruit coulis in the bottom of a glass of champagne as a welcome drink at dinner parties.

250g (9oz) chosen berries; strawberries, blackberries, raspberries, blueberries or mulberries (if you are lucky enough to have some in your backyard)

6 tablespoons (120ml/4fl oz) sugar syrup (see Index for easy sugar syrup preparation)

In a medium saucepan, combine berries and sugar, then bring to simmer over medium heat. Simmer until fruit just starts to break down then remove from heat, cool and puree. Take a fine sieve and rub mixture through and serve as desired.

Store in the freezer for up to 6 weeks.

or

Another way I have been taught to make berry coulis is super simple. Spread your berries of choice over a baking tray, and then sprinkle a generous tablespoon of icing sugar, leave for about an hour, and then process all in a blender and voila! The sugar draws the juice out of the fruit. Just remember to sieve, if necessary, to remove any seeds.

From the Heart

These are the kind of sweets that are offered over garden fences. Make a loved one feel special or welcome a new neighbour (we like to think people still do this). Send a warm cuddle in a delicious treat—these are sweets that put smiles on faces.

Lemon Madeira

Serves 6–8
Preparation time: 15–20 minutes
Cooking time: 25 minutes

This cake is lovely and you can make it your own recipe, in so many ways. Dress it up with a Limoncello Glaze or Candied Citrus, Spiced Ginger Cream, Lemon Mousse (see Index), or any one of the gorgeous frosts or Chantilly Creams found in the Bling chapter. Enjoy the choices.

250g (9oz) butter, softened

200g (7oz) caster (superfine) sugar

2 lemons, zested and juiced

250g (9oz) self-raising (self-rising) flour

1 teaspoon baking powder

5 eggs, lightly beaten

Preheat oven 170°C (335°F/Gas Mark 3). Prepare two 20cm-round (8in) cake tins, by greasing with butter on base and sides.

In a mixing bowl, combine butter and sugar, mix until light and fluffy, then add lemon zest. Set aside. In another medium bowl, add flour and baking powder, using a whisk to combine.

To the butter mixture, add eggs gradually and add about 1 tablepoon of flour after each egg. This should prevent curdling. Beat well, after each egg.

Gently fold in flour mixture until combined. Then add lemon juice and gently fold until the mixture looks nice and soft.

Gently spoon the mixture into the two pans evenly, smooth over the top gently. This recipe is worth the care.

Bake for 25 minutes in the centre of the oven. Set your timer. When cooked, remove from oven, leave to cool for 5 minutes, and then remove carefully onto a wire cake rack to cool. Dress your cake as desired.

For the Blackberry, Elderflower and Lemon Mousse Trifle (see Index) carefully remove tops off cakes. This will allow the cake to absorb all the wonderful ingredients of your trifle.

Orange Yoghurt Syrup Cake

Serves 16

Preparation time: 20 minutes

Cooking time: 40 minutes in loaf pans (50 minutes in cake pan)

Makes 2 loaf pans, one for me and one for you, or one large cake. One for me!

Drenched in syrup, this cake is highly addictive. It is moist, spongy and oh-so-satisfyingly dense.

CAKE

300g (10½oz) unsalted butter

300g (10½ oz) raw (demerara) sugar

3 cups (450g/15oz) plain (all-purpose) flour

1 tablespoon bicarbonate of soda (baking soda)

2–3 teaspoons orange zest

½ cup (130g/4oz) plain, unsweetened yoghurt

½ cup (125g/4oz) sour cream

½ cup (125ml/4oz) orange juice

Pinch of salt

3 eggs, beaten

1 teaspoon vanilla paste

Butter, for greasing two loaf pans

SYRUP

½ cup (125ml/4oz) orange juice

2 tablespoons (40g/1½oz) raw (demerara) sugar

1 tablespoon (20ml/⅔oz) lemon juice

2 tablespoons (40ml/ 1½oz) orange liqueur (Triple sec/Cointreau)

Preheat oven 180°C (350°F/Gas Mark 4). Butter two loaf pans roughly 20 x 10 x 6cm (8 x 4 x 2½in) or one large cake tin 22 x 5cm (9 x 2in).

Find four medium bowls suitable for the following steps:

Cream butter and sugar and set aside.

Combine flour, bicarbonate of soda and zest. Set aside.

Combine yoghurt, sour cream, juice and salt. Set aside.

Beat the three eggs with vanilla. Set aside.

In the bowl with the butter and sugar, slowly add a little of the dry mixture, the yoghurt mixture and the egg mixture until all is combined. Once everything is added, place the well-combined dough into prepared pans and bake for 40 minutes or until a bamboo skewer comes out clean.

Let cake(s) cool for 10 minutes before turning out of pan(s) and onto plates. Let cool while preparing the syrup.

Combine all syrup ingredients in a small saucepan and bring to boil for 4 minutes. Simmer for about 4 minutes, uncovered. Take the syrup and pour slowly over the warm cake(s), so it soaks through and then leave to cool to room temperature. Dress with Candied Citrus (see Bling chapter). Slice and serve.

You can convert this cake into a sensational poppy seed cake by adding ½ to ⅓ cup of poppy seeds to the syrup mix.

This cake is also lovely and simple without the syrup, if you are pressed for time.

You can also substitute this fruit syrup for the liqueur glaze of Limoncello Glaze.

Apricot Baklava

Approximately 20 pieces

I love baklava. Turkish, Greek or Persian, I don't mind. Layer upon layer upon layer, it is rich and moreish. I couldn't resist this flavour combination—I thought it a marriage made in heaven. If you would like to make a traditional version, just remove the apricot and double the nuts.For Greek-style baklava use walnuts, for Turkish use pistachios. Either will result in sticky, gooey yumminess to share. If you are conscious of the fat content, reduce the ghee and brush sparingly between filo sheets.

225g (8oz) ghee, warmed (butter is ok if ghee can't be found)

375g (13oz) apricot jam (buy a 500g (17½oz) jar, as you use the jam in the syrup as well)

1 large egg, beaten

¼ cup (60ml/2fl oz) honey

1 teaspoon ground cardamom

½ teaspoon ground cinnamon

½ teaspoon ground nutmeg

20 sheets filo (phyllo) pastry (about one box), thawed

250g (9oz) pistachios, finely crushed (my choice) or walnuts (use a coffee grinder or food processor for best results)

SYRUP

½ cup (125ml/4fl oz) honey

½ cup (125g/4fl oz) apricot jam

Squeeze of lemon juice

Preheat oven 150°C (300°F/Gas Mark 2).

Prepare a baking dish—I use a glass dish 30 x 20cm (12 x 8in). Brush it with ghee, set aside. Fill another with just water. This is to keep the environment moist in the oven while cooking, so any cake pan will do here.

Combine the apricot jam, egg, honey and spices. Combine well and set aside. Take out the packet of filo pastry, which should be approximately 20 sheets. Keep a clean, damp tea towel over filo, when on the kitchen bench, to prevent it from drying out.

Continues...

Lay down the first sheet of filo into a baking pan. Brush with warm ghee. Repeat for 4 sheets.

Then lay a thin layer of apricot mixture, evenly distributing over the pastry.

Sprinkle with pistachios. Lay another filo, brush with ghee. Repeat for 4 sheets. Try to keep the process neat and ensure all your edges are coated in ghee.

Lay another serving of apricot mixture, nuts and another 4 buttered layers of filo. Repeat again until all the apricot mixture and nuts are finished off.

Finish with 4 layers of buttered filo on top. Score the baklava into desired shapes for serving. DO NOT CUT ALL THE WAY THROUGH. For triangular shapes, cut the baklava into rectangular shapes, and then cut those rectangular shapes diagonally in half. Or serve as you please, it won't taste any different.

Place the baklava on the middle oven tray. Place the pan of water on the bottom tray in the oven. This will prevent the baklava from drying out. Bake for 45 minutes.

To make the syrup, combine honey, jam and lemon in a small saucepan and warm through over a low heat.

Remove the baklava from the oven and cut into slices now all the way through. Pour the syrup evenly over the baklava, allowing it to soak through.

Once cooked, place in the fridge overnight. The flavour intensifies and it is well worth waiting for. In my house though, half goes after cooking and half goes into the fridge to devour the next day.

Honey and Peach Butter

Makes about 2L (70fl oz)

Preparation: 10 minutes

Cooking time: 2 hours

Reduce the recipe if you want a lesser amount, otherwise bottle up this yummy goodness. This recipe makes a lovely gift—keep some for yourself and give freely to others. Gorgeous on toast, mixed in a Bircher muesli or porridge, this is sweet bliss.

8–10 peaches, washed, skinned, pitted and cubed (alternatively, use 1kg (2lb 4oz) sliced, canned peaches. No need to cube, these will break down in the cooking process)

2 tablespoons (40g/1½oz) ground cinnamon
1 teaspoon ground nutmeg
6 cloves
1 cup (250ml/9fl oz) honey

Put peaches in a large heavy-based saucepan and add ⅓ cup (100ml /2¾fl oz) filtered water. Cook over low heat, stirring regularly until the mixture has turned brown. This could take about 2 hours.

Add spices and the honey, remove from stovetop and leave to cool. Meanwhile, sterilise your jars.

Pour the mixture into jars and remove the clove buds. Refrigerate.

Maple Pecan Pie

Serves 6

This is an all-time favourite winter dessert in our family. I love the mounds of leaves that fall, waiting for happy children to fly into and bury themselves in. But despite that, at our place in winter, the pecan trees are forgiven because of the childhood memories they create of leaf stacks and warm pecan pie and a dollop of whipped vanilla cream. If you like, substitute maple syrup for traditional dark corn syrup. You may also like to try walnuts or macadamias for something different instead of pecans.

1 quantity of Sweet Shortcrust Pastry (see Index)

FILLING
4 eggs, beaten
¾ cup (180ml/6fl oz) maple syrup

2 tablespoons (40ml/1½fl oz) lemon juice
1 teaspoon cinnamon
1 teaspoon nutmeg
2 teaspoons vanilla paste
2 cups (500g/17½oz) pecans, chopped

Preheat oven to 180°C (350°F/ Gas Mark 4). Prepare pastry.

Beat all the ingredients together, except the nuts, until light and fluffy. Set aside. Take the crushed nuts and distribute evenly in the pie shell.

Now pour filling into baked piecrust and bake for 30–40 minutes or until a bamboo skewer comes out clean when placed in the centre of the pie.

Remove from oven and allow to cool for at least 30 minutes, before serving at room temperature with your preferred topping. Can also be served cold with ice cream, whipped cream or Cinnamon or Chantilly Cream (see Index).

Lemon Curd

Makes 1½ cups
Preparation/Cooking time: 20 minutes

My nan used to make lemon curd, or butter as some may prefer to call it. I remember there was always an announcement in our house when she was making it and there was such excitement to follow. I loved to collect and prepare jars for her. I'd watch and wait for a delicious serving on toast that always followed. With this recipe, you might start a tradition. Double this recipe if making for another as well. You can use this in the Lemon Mousse or the Blackberry, Elderflower and Lemon Mousse Trifle.

2 eggs, beaten

50g (1¾oz) unsalted butter

1 cup (250ml/9fl oz) honey

2 lemons, juiced, zest of 1 lemon

Place ingredients in a medium bowl and then place bowl over a medium saucepan of boiling water Whisk constantly until the mixture thickens, being careful not to burn. Remove from heat. This should take about 15 minutes.

Cool slightly and then pour into sterilised jars.

You can pour this over a warm cake or gingerbread. It will refrigerate for up to a week in a bowl covered with cling film. If placed into sterilised jars, the curd will last up to two months in the fridge.

Killer Banana and Chocolate Bread

Serves 6

The combination of ripe bananas with dark chocolate is almost unbeatable in my books. There's a reason why banana bread is a staple in so many families throughout the years. This recipe is a tricked-up version. When you bake this beauty it fills the house with the most gorgeous aroma, which is almost as rewarding as actually eating this bread...almost.

6 ripe bananas

1½ cups (225g/8oz) self-raising (self-rising) flour

1 teaspoon bicarbonate of soda (baking soda)

100g (3½oz) butter

90g (3oz) caster (superfine) sugar

2 large eggs

1 teaspoon vanilla extract or paste

90g (3oz) sour cream

¾ cup (100g/3½oz) dark (semi-sweet) chocolate, 70% cocoa, chopped into chunks

Handful of walnuts, pecans or macadamia nuts

45g (1½oz) brown sugar

Preheat oven to 180°C (350°F/Gas Mark 4). Butter and then line all sides of two 20 x 10cm (8 x 4in) loaf tins with greaseproof paper.

Mash three of the bananas. Sift together the flour and bicarbonate of soda in a bowl.

In a large bowl, use an electric beater to cream the butter and caster sugar until pale, light and fluffy. Stir in the eggs, one at a time. Fold in the vanilla and mashed bananas.

Combine the mashed banana mix into the flour mix, being careful not to over-stir. Slice the remaining three bananas into big chunks. Fold in the banana pieces, sour cream and chunks of chocolate and nuts, again being careful not to over-mix. Pour cake batter (which should be very thick) into prepared loaf tin. Sprinkle with brown sugar.

Bake the two tins for 40 minutes. For one big single loaf, bake for 30 minutes at 180°C (350°F), covering the top of the cake with a greaseproof paper. Then reduce the temperature to 160°C (320°F) and bake for another 30–40 minutes or until it's firm to touch. A skewer inserted into the middle should come out clean.

Moist Carrot Cake

Serves 16
Preparation time: 20 minutes
Cooking time: 50 minutes
Gluten-free

I love a good carrot cake. They are wholesome and comforting. It makes a fitting birthday cake for a friend. You can modify this recipe to suit your tastes and pantry limitations—an oldie but a goodie.
On special occasions, dress it up with Cream Cheese Frosting (see Index) add a few extra chopped walnuts and crushed praline, for something spectacular! Otherwise, enjoy just as it is, and if you have children or grand kiddies, omit the nuts and it makes a great addition to the children's lunchbox for the week. It is so tempting it will be hard to stop at one piece.

2 cups (300g/10½oz) pre-made gluten-free plain
    (all-purpose) flour
2 cups (400g/14oz) raw (demerara) sugar
¼ cup (25g/¾oz) chopped walnuts (or other)
¼ cup (45g/1½oz) sultanas (or raisins)
1 teaspoon baking powder

2 teaspoon ground cinnamon
¼ teaspoon ground nutmeg
¼ teaspoon ground cloves
4 eggs
4 cups (320g/11oz) carrot, grated
1 cup (250ml/9fl oz) vegetable oil
2 teaspoons vanilla paste (or extract)

Preheat oven to 180°C (350°F/Gas Mark 4).

    Grease a 33 x 23 x 5cm (13 x 9 x 2in) rectangular baking pan (or a square 25 x 25 x 5cm (10 x 10 x 2in) pan), and set aside.

    In a large mixing bowl, combine all dry ingredients with a whisk and set aside.

    In a medium bowl, beat your eggs and add grated carrot, oil and vanilla. Mix well.

    Combine wet ingredients with dry ingredients and then pour batter into a greased pan. Bake for 50–60 minutes, or until a bamboo skewer comes out clean when stuck in the middle of the cake.

Traditional with a Twist

Take a trip down memory lane with this collection of traditional and heartfelt favourites. Some of these desserts remind and connect us to loved ones past and present. We know every family has its own rich history—here you can delight in memories of sweet times.

Italian Mamma's Tiramisu

Serves 8

One of my favourite people that I met during my time on MasterChef was Adele. We called her the Italian Mamma and she was, without doubt, the heart of the MasterChef household. She has shared her famous tiramisu recipe with us. A gratifying tiramisu uses good Savoiardi biscuits, which are an Italian sponge biscuit. With Adele's permission I have halved the Savoiardi biscuits as I find them to be quite thick. Being an absolute chocolate fiend, I have added more chocolate and reduced the amount of sugar in the original recipe.

5 eggs, separated

120g (4oz) caster (superfine) sugar

350g (12oz) mascarpone cheese

300ml (10½fl oz) fresh brewed coffee or 300ml (10½fl oz) hot water and 6 tablespoons instant coffee

¼ cup sugar, extra

2 tablespoons Marsala

10 sponge biscuits (Savoiardi)

150g (5oz) dark (semi-sweet), 70% cocoa, chocolate, chopped up into slivers

Beat egg yolks with the sugar until sugar has dissolved and mix is light and fluffy. Add the mascarpone and mix in well. Whisk egg whites in a clean glass bowl using an electric beater until soft peaks form, then fold into mascarpone mixture.

Put warm coffee into a shallow dish, add sugar and Marsala and stir to dissolve sugar. Turn your Savoiardi biscuits on their side and, using a sharp knife, cut them in half to make them very slender (the same shape as original just thinner).

Quickly and carefully dip half of the biscuits in coffee, one at a time, so that they are soaked. Then place them in the base of individual dishes or one bigger if you prefer. Spread with mascarpone mix and then dip the other half of the biscuits in coffee, one at a time and place these soaked biscuits on top of mascarpone mix. Finish with a layer of mascarpone smoothing the layer and then sprinkle your chunks of chocolate on top.

Refrigerate for two to three hours and you are ready to delight your family or your guests.

traditional with a twist

Blackberry, Elderflower and Lemon Mousse Trifle

Serves 12

In true 1970s retro style, comes this trifle invention, with colours of lemon and blackberry—fitting for any special occasion and a stunning end to any meal.

LEMON MADEIRA

Use our Lemon Madeira recipe (see Index) but if you're pressed for time, buy a store-bought madeira cake or plain sponge.

ELDERFLOWER JELLY

(You can make this jelly and eat it on its own. It serves 10 and is lovely served with whipped cream.)

5 sheets leaf gelatine, soaked

170ml (6fl oz) elderflower cordial

2 heaped tablespoons (50g/1¾oz) caster (super-fine) sugar

1 lemon, juiced

600ml (19fl oz) lemonade, chilled

LEMON MOUSSE

600ml (21fl oz) thickened cream

2 tablespoons (40g/1½oz) lemon curd (either purchased or made fresh in advance see Index)

TO ASSEMBLE

80ml (2½fl oz) Limoncello (Italian lemon liqueur) or elderflower cordial

500g (17½oz) blackberries

100g (3½oz) milk or dark chocolate (room temperature, leave out for an hour to make chocolate curls)

ELDERFLOWER JELLY

For the jelly, take your gelatine leaves and soak them in a little cold water, for about a minute. Fill a saucepan with water, place over a medium heat and bring to a simmer. Fit a bowl over the saucepan and add the cordial to the bowl.

Continues...

Drain the gelatine and add to the cordial, stirring constantly until the mixture becomes syrup.

Add caster sugar then lemon juice and stir until sugar dissolves. Remove the bowl from the heat and set aside.

Pour the lemonade into the cordial mix.

If serving this jelly as a separate dessert, pour into a bowl and set in the fridge. This should take about an hour. Otherwise, follow the trifle assembly instructions below.

LEMON MOUSSE

(You can use this separately as a layer filling on a Lemon Sponge, just reduce recipe by half.)

Combine whipped cream and lemon curd to make mousse. Easy!

TO ASSEMBLE TRIFLE

Use a 20–25cm (8–10in) trifle bowl (a round bowl with straight edges) and pour in the elderflower jelly. I prefer the pedestal trifle bowls for more wow factor. Add the berries and refrigerate until set.

When jelly is set, take the lemon sponge (or other) and layer on top of the jelly. Pour your choice of Limoncello (or elderflower cordial), over the top of the sponge. I like to use a clean spray bottle and spray the sponge for even distribution.

Place the Lemon Mousse over the soaked sponge.

Now place the other portion of the berries in the centre of the trifle, covering roughly three-quarters of the surface. Place in the fridge while you prepare the final garnish.

To make chocolate curls, take the slightly softened chocolate and place on bench, over foil or baking paper. Stand directly in front and, working from the top and sides of the chocolate bar, run the peeler toward you, peeling the chocolate into curls. If you choose to use dark chocolate, it may take a little practice, and if it is all proving too painful, just chop finely on a slight diagonal to get long strips of chocolate. Using tongs, transfer the curls into an airtight container or place directly on top of your trifle.

Just before serving, top your trifle with the other half of blackberries and lashings of shaved chocolate.

Apricot Tarte Tatin

Serves 4
Preparation time: 20 minutes
Cooking time: 20 minutes

Warning! You will need to be extremely disciplined around this sweet treat. Although tarte tatin is traditionally made with apple, experiment with plums, figs, nectarines or peaches. Serve with crème fraîche or ice cream. You'll be hard pressed to beat this simple winter warmer.

4 apricots or 1 medium tin of apricot halves (tinned work really well in this recipe)
1 sheet puff pastry
70g (2¼oz) caster (superfine) sugar

40g (1½oz) butter, melted
1 tub of your favourite vanilla ice cream, crème fraîche or the Cinnamon Cream (see Index)

Preheat oven to 190°C (375°F/Gas Mark 5). If using canned apricots, drain apricots and let them dry on some paper towel. You want them to be as dry as possible. If using fresh apricots halve and deseed them, then place them on paper towel.

Place a 20cm (8in) oven-friendly non-stick frypan over a medium heat and scatter half of the sugar over the base. Once sugar starts to caramelise, add the rest of the sugar and stir until it has all melted and is a lovely, golden caramel colour.

Add melted butter and whisk to combine, making a caramel. Don't worry if it splits, keep going. Take the pan off the heat and place as many apricots (curved side down) as will fit neatly over the base of the pan.

Using a knife, cut a circle of puff pastry that is slightly bigger than the frypan used for the caramel. Score the middle of the pastry so that the steam can escape. Cover the pan with puff pastry and tuck the edges in. Bake in the oven until the pastry is golden brown and puffed up (approx. 20–25 mins).

Take out of the oven and let it stand for a few minutes.

To serve, place a plate that is larger than the pan over the top and then carefully turn the tart upside down, so that it lands on the plate. Remove the pan gently and be careful of the hot caramel as it can burn you. Serve with ice cream for sheer bliss.

traditional with a twist

Strawberry Yoghurt Cheesecake

Serves 8–12 (big slices in my house)
Preparation time: 20–30 minutes

This is one of my all-time favourite desserts. All credit here goes to my culinary hero—my mum, Carole Seymour. It took years to get this recipe and while I have now made this numerous times, I never tire of it. I modify it often, as does my daughter (that's the beauty of it). Strawberry is my choice of yoghurt, cherry a close second. My kids jump up and down at the whisper that one may be on its way, planned for a Sunday treat.
Note: *For the vegetarian or additive sensitive, use Agar Agar as an alternative to animal derived gelatine.*

BASE

1 packet (400g/14oz) digestive biscuits of your
    choice
80–100g/2½–3½oz butter, melted (some biscuits
    are more absorbent than others)
Butter, for greasing 20cm (10in) spring-form tin

FILLING

2½ cups (650g/22¾fl oz) flavoured yoghurt of choice
    or 4 x 170g (6oz) tubs of flavoured yoghurt (you
    can use plain, unsweetened yoghurt and add a
    coulis here, just use 2½ cups)
1 cup (200g/7oz) raw (demerara) sugar
250g (9oz) cream cheese
2 tablespoons (40g/1½oz) powdered gelatine (or
    agar agar (see Glossary))

BASE

Prepare a spring form pan, cover the base with greaseproof paper or foil and grease over the top and sides of pan with a little butter.

Using a food processor crush the biscuits or place biscuits in a large zip-lock bag and roll a rolling pin over the contents until they resemble coarse breadcrumbs.

Continues...

traditional with a twist

In a small saucepan, melt the butter over a low heat. Combine the two ingredients and press into the base and sides of the prepared spring-form pan.

Place the prepared base in the freezer for 10 minutes, until you add the filling.

FILLING

Blend the yoghurt, sugar and cream cheese in a blender. Take the gelatine powder and ⅓ cup (2fl oz) hot water and mix well, to avoid lumps. When fully dissolved add to blended yoghurt mix and blend again. At this point don't walk off—gelatine sets REALLY quickly!

Remove the pan from freezer and add the filling. Return to fridge to set.

When set, remove and run a knife around the edge of pan, release the spring and carefully remove the ring over the top of cake.

Cut to desired serving sizes and serve alone or with Berry Coulis (see Index).

Cinnamon Ice Cream

Serves 4

Preparation time: 15 minutes

Cooking time: 30 minutes plus 35 minutes churning

Freeze: 4 hours

I am happiest when sitting cross-legged on the couch, eating a sizeable bowl of this fine sweet. The Orange and Nutmeg Pudding (see Index) should welcome this ice cream any day of the week. You will need an ice cream maker for this recipe.

2 tablespoons cinnamon (or wattleseed), finely ground

400ml (14fl oz) pouring cream

100ml (3½fl oz) milk

5 egg yolks

70g (2¼oz) caster (superfine) sugar

40ml (1½fl oz) glucose syrup

Combine cream, milk and cinnamon (or wattleseed) in a saucepan and bring gently to just below the boil, then remove from heat and leave to infuse.

Meanwhile, whisk egg yolks, sugar and glucose syrup until pale and creamy. Gradually add in the hot cream mixture, whisking to combine, then pour this back into the saucepan. Stir continuously with a wooden spoon, over a low heat, until the mixture thickens enough to coat the back of a wooden spoon (about 84°C/180°F on a digital thermometer).

Strain the mixture through a fine sieve into a bowl that is sitting in a larger bowl of ice. Stir till cool and then transfer to an ice cream maker for approximately 30 minutes until smooth and frozen. Once ice cream has been churned, transfer to a container and freeze.

Coconut Sago with Chilli Mango Sorbet

Serves 4

Preparation/Cooking time: 35 minutes

To satiate our passion for food and snowboarding, I followed my younger sister, Erin, my chef extraordinaire Kylie Craig and my friend Michelle Spense to Canada, before Erin passed away in 2001. Erin loved sago and this recipe is one she consumed at great speed. I loved her dearly and she was my best friend. This one is for you Ezzza. We miss you.

Notes: *This can also be made with pineapple, nectarines, mulberries or bananas. Can also be served with the Nectarine and Honey Ice Cream (see Index). You can also add a chilli to the nectarine ice cream.*

One quantity of Mango and Coconut Sorbet (see Index), for serving

¼ birdseye chilli, finely chopped

120g (4¼oz) tapioca or sago

5 tablespoons palm sugar or caster sugar

3 cups (750ml) coconut milk

2 limes, juiced

1 cup coconut cream

GARNISH

Coconut flakes, toasted

Kaffir lime leaves, finely shredded

Make one quantity of mango sorbet. Add the chilli for an added heat to cold ice cream.

To make the sago, combine all ingredients, except coconut cream, in a saucepan over medium heat. Bring the mix to the boil and simmer for 25 minutes or until the tapioca is translucent and the mix is thick, stirring constantly. Stir the coconut cream through when you take off heat. You can make the sago ahead of time and keep in the fridge till you are ready to serve.

Just before serving, reheat your sago mixture and pour into 4 simple, elegant glasses. Place some sorbet in a beautiful bowl next to the sago and throw your garnish into small separate bowls too. You're now ready to eat this tasty treat.

traditional with a twist

Mango and Coconut Sorbet

Serves 4

Preparation/Cooking time: 5 minutes

This wonderful sorbet is made with 100 per cent raw fruit and is utterly delicious. This process can be used with other sweet fruit, such as nectarines, pineapple, mulberries, bananas, etc. Steer clear of watery fruit such as citrus, grapes, strawberries, as you will end up with a fruit ice. It is perfect for hot summer days and balmy nights. If you want to be really adventurous, you could try using some chilli in this recipe for a sensational contrast between the cold sorbet and the hot chilli. It is so quick to make, so you can spend more time with the people you love.

Note: *If you want to make this recipe low in fat, just leave out the coconut cream.*

3 mangoes

¾ cup (180ml/6fl oz) coconut cream

2 tablespoons lime juice, freshly squeezed

2 tablespoons (40ml/1½fl oz) honey

Handful of mint leaves

Chilli (optional)

Peel and slice mangoes into small pieces and freeze in a container for several hours or overnight. Can be stored for up to 3 months.

When you are ready to make this delicious dessert, remove from freezer and allow mangoes to partially thaw. The mangoes should not fully thaw and should still have ice crystals in them.

Place partially thawed mangoes, coconut cream, lime juice, honey and mint leaves in blender and puree until smooth. Serve in a beautiful glass and garnish with mint or basil leaves.

Warm Pumpkin Pie with Spiced Ginger Cream

Serves 8

Preparation time: 20 minutes

Cooking time: 35 minutes

I don't know how old I was when I first tried it, but I remember thinking, how can pumpkin taste so good? These days I love it with spiced ginger cream on top, but it is gorgeous and mouth-watering just by itself.

PASTRY

1½ cups (225g/8oz) plain (all-purpose)
or wholemeal flour

3 tablespoons (60g/2oz) raw (demerara) sugar

125g (4oz) unsalted butter, chilled, cut into cubes

1 large egg

FILLING

500g (17½oz) pumpkin, cooked

125g (4oz) brown sugar

2 eggs

1 teaspoon vanilla extract

2 teaspoons cinnamon

1 teaspoon ground ginger

½ teaspoon nutmeg

300ml (1½ cups/10¼fl oz) cream

1½ tablespoons (30ml/1oz) brandy

Preheat oven to 180°C (350°F/Gas Mark 4).

To make the pastry, combine flour and sugar then add butter, working it in with your fingers until the mixture is crumbly. Set aside.

In a small bowl, beat the egg, then add to the flour mix, stirring with a fork. Press dough evenly into a 28cm (11in) tart pan, with removable bottom and set aside. Prepare filling.

In a bowl, blend together the pumpkin (drain well), sugar, egg, spices, cream and brandy until smooth. Pour the filling into a pastry case and bake for 35–40 minutes or until set. Now prepare the Spiced Ginger Cream.

traditional with a twist

Spiced Ginger Cream

This is delicious. Not only is it a great addition to pumpkin pie, you can use it on top of a vanilla cupcake, pound cake or simple sponge (store-bought even). Try on the Lemon Madeira or the Orange Yoghurt Syrup Cake (see Index). Mmm...

375ml (13 oz) cream cheese
50g (1¾oz) sour cream
2 teaspoons maple syrup
125g (4oz/¼lb) icing (confectioners') sugar, sifted
1 teaspoon ground cinnamon

1 teaspoon ground nutmeg
35g (1¼oz) glacé ginger, finely chopped (double the quantity if you would like to use as a garnish on cream)

Beat together the cream cheese and sour cream. Add maple syrup, icing sugar and spices.
Fold in glacé ginger and serve.

Brazilian Caramelised Bananas

Serves 2

Preparation/Cooking time: 10 minutes

Bananas are used often in Brazilian cuisine and are most commonly fried with the addition of one of my favourite spices—cinnamon. Cinnamon trees grow in the tropical zones of Brazil and this spice has become a household favourite not just in Brazil but throughout the world. You can make the Brazilian Bananas in a flash and they make a welcome partner to the Elvis Presley Parfait or Cinnamon Cream (see Index).

⅓ caster (superfine) sugar	3 tablespoons butter
¼ cup (60ml/2fl oz) thickened cream	4 bananas, peeled and cut in half lengthways
Pinch of cinnamon	

Using a medium frypan, place the sugar in the pan over a medium heat. As soon as you see the sugar start to melt stir, ensuring the sugar on the outside of the pot doesn't burn. You may see some of the sugar clump up, but just continue to heat until all of the sugar has melted and turns a deep caramel colour. Add cream and cinnamon and stir for 2 minutes or until combined.

Grab another medium fry pan, cook your butter and bananas over a medium heat. Flip your bananas after a few minutes once they are golden brown and cook for a few more minutes. Place bananas on serving plates. Drizzle all of that lovely caramel over the top of the bananas.

Karla's Citrus Tart

Serves 10

My childhood friend Karla has a wonderful garden with magnificent lemon and lime trees, from which she makes an insanely good tart. This lovely tart is zesty, zingy but well-balanced by the creaminess of the crème fraîche. We have gone for a 20cm (10in) removable base tart tin. A deep-sized quiche tin the same size will work as well. If you use a tart tin, you will have around 200ml (7oz) of the citrus cream left over, which you can pour into a mould and bake as individual custards. As soon as it comes out of the oven, cut a slice, custard oozing, and, before you know it, you may well have 'accidentally' eaten half of the tart. It is best served warm.

Note: Put your flour and food processor container in the freezer well ahead of time to make sure that you keep your pastry as cold as possible. Pastry loves the cold. You can also fill a bowl with ice and water to dip your hands in to keep them cold when handling the pastry. Make sure you don't overwork the pastry. For the softest and most delicate pastry, work quickly, as the pastry becomes quite fragile as it heats up. Handle it as carefully as you would a baby.

1 quantity of Maggie Beer's Sour Cream Pastry
   (see Index)

FILLING
75g (2 ½oz) caster sugar
6 large egg yolks

¼ cup (60ml/2fl oz) lime juice
2 tablespoons lemon juice
1 lime and 1 lemon, rind finely grated
400ml (12fl oz) crème fraîche or sour cream (to
   save money)
Icing sugar (to dust)

Make pastry according to instructions.

To make filling, turn the oven temperature down to 180°C (350°F/Gas Mark 4). Beat the sugar, eggs, juice and rind together until smooth, then fold in crème fraîche. Fill the warm pastry case with your mixture and bake in oven for 25 minutes or until set.

When cooled, you can dust this beauty with icing sugar. Serve with Chantilly Cream or Crème Fraîche Ice Cream (see Index).

traditional with a twist

PS I Love You

Seduce your partner, lover or current squeeze with this collection that's as unique as you are. Aphrodisiacs are bountiful and plenty in this saucy chapter of goodness. Tasty wines to match, this is a heady recipe to seduce your lover.

Bittersweet Chocolate and Pomegranate Tarts

Makes 8

Preparation time: 30 minutes

Let's face it—most of us are juggling many commitments these days. This recipe avoids pastry making, hot ovens and, best of all, it is probably going to appeal to even the most discerning of tastebuds. Garnish options of summer strawberries, pomegranate jewels, spicy cherries, blood orange or my cardamom-spiced oranges, hit this sweet treat with a good dose of acidity and balance the dessert well.

Feel free to take the chocolate out of the base to make it gluten-free or use a gluten-free chocolate. Please use your favourite good-quality chocolate (I use Lindt 70% cocoa). Good chocolate makes the world of difference to this dessert.

BASE
70g (2¼oz) dark (semisweet), 70% cocoa, chocolate

1½ cups pecans

4 medjool dates

CREAM
450g (16oz) crème fraîche or sour cream

45g (1½ oz) brown sugar

TOPPING OPTIONS
1 pomegranate, jewels removed

1 punnet of fresh local strawberries (top off and quartered)

1 quantity of spicy cherries (see Index)

1 blood or navel orange, peeled, pith removed and sliced in between the orange segments

1 quantity of Cardamom-spiced Oranges (see Index)

BASE
Blitz the chocolate and ½ cup of the pecans in a food processor until you have small chunks. Set aside.

Continues...

To make tartlet shells, scoop about 2 tablespoons of the crust into about 8 x 8cm (3¼in) bottomless tart tins. Use your fingertips to firmly press the crust into the tin, leaving a cavity in the centre to hold the cream. Place in the freezer for about 4–8 hours to set.

CREAM

Mix the crème fraîche or sour cream and brown sugar together in a bowl. Take the tart cases out of the freezer and scoop 1 tablespoon of the cream into each tartlet shell and place in the fridge for a few hours to set.

Serve tarts on plates and top with a garnish of your choice. You can cover these with cling film and put into the fridge for later if you have the discipline.

Serve with Pinot Noir or Zinfandel.

Vanilla Bean Figs

Preparation/Cooking time: 15 minutes

Cooked figs have been used throughout history in North Africa and the Middle East as a sweetener instead of sugar. They are onto a good thing as these little parcels of deliciousness are also high in potassium, iron, plant calcium and fibre. A scrumptious way to sweeten other desserts, throw on top of your morning porridge or eat them on their own. Bottle them, throw on a ribbon and a little tag and you have a heartfelt gift for a friend.

2 cups (375g/13¼oz) dried figs (do not buy the soft and juicy ones—these have preservatives in them)

⅓ cup (70g/2¼oz) caster sugar
1 vanilla bean, split in half and seeds scraped or 2 teaspoons vanilla bean paste

Place all ingredients, plus 3 cups water in a small saucepan over a low-medium heat and bring to the boil. Remove from heat and allow the flavours to infuse for at least 30 minutes.

If you want to serve the figs as soon as possible, you can reheat them after 30 minutes. Otherwise, transfer to a sterilised glass jar to store in the fridge and allow the favours to develop further. When ready to use, you can either eat straight from the jar or reheat for serious goodness.

Serve with Cinnamon Cream or Ice Cream or crème fraîche with some syrup drizzled over the top.

Serve with Pinot Noir or Pedro Ximenez Sherry.

You Make Me Blush Raspberry Cashew Cups

Serves 8

Preparation/Cooking time: 25 minutes

Gluten-free

If you're thinking of treating your lover (or anyone else for that matter) to a tasty treat full of love and nutrition, then this is the dessert for you. Whip it up in a jiffy and watch them swoon.

RASPBERRY CASHEW CREAM

2 cups cashews, raw unsalted

4 cups frozen raspberries, thawed

½ cup agave syrup, honey or sugar syrup

2 cups coconut milk

100ml (3¼ fl oz) lemon juice

½ cup coconut oil, refined or coconut butter (you can leave this out if need be)

½ teaspoon salt

GARNISH

Handful each of fresh raspberries and strawberries, chopped in half

Optional: 1 red plum, halved, seed removed, Uncle Bruce's Extravaganza or Crème Fraîche Ice Cream (see Index), rose petals, edible flowers, glass balls (made very small) (see Index), macadamia or Brazil nuts, roughly chopped

Blend Cashew Cream ingredients in a high-powered blender. Strain the mixture through a fine sieve to remove raspberry seeds. Pour cream into a bowl, cover with cling film and refrigerate for a few hours.

To serve your lover extravagantly, grab a beautiful bowl and place in a plum half or two, a quenelle of ice cream, rose petals, edible flowers and mini glass balls (or any combination).

For the easy version, throw a few nuts into the bottom of some glasses, pour in the raspberry cashew cream and place in the fridge (softer) or freezer (ice-creamy), whatever you prefer, for a few hours and then devour. Freeze well ahead of time and take out approximately 45 minutes before serving. It's best when served semi-frozen. Garnish with some fresh raspberries and strawberries or a handful of chopped nuts. Serve with Verdicchio or Riesling.

ps I love you

Lime Dumplings with Mango

Serves 8

Preparation time: 15 minutes

Cooking time: 20 minutes

Gluten-free

Traditional Chinese dumplings are usually served without any filling. However the addition of a crunchy nut on the inside takes this dumpling to a whole new level—it's all about the texture baby! The dumplings are neutral in flavour and are beautiful served piping hot with the sweet and tangy lime syrup. Glutinous rice flour is fine for those with a wheat intolerance. Glutinous means sticky.

DUMPLINGS

250g (8¾oz) glutinous rice flour (buy this from an Asian grocer and yes it must be glutinous rice flour, not just rice flour)

¾ cup water (you may need a little extra depending on the flour)

Handful of macadamia or Brazil nuts, roughly chopped

LIME SYRUP

½ cup caster sugar

1 lime, for zest and juice

50ml (1¾fl oz) water

GARNISH

2 mangoes

Handful of shredded coconut

Optional: a few kaffir lime leaves, finely shredded (buy these from your local green grocer)

To make dumplings, first bring a large pot of water on the boil. Using a big bowl, mix the glutinous rice flour with ¾ cup of water until it forms a smooth paste and it doesn't stick to your hands anymore. Grab small handfuls of the mix and divide it equally into small balls (should make approximately 25).

Continues...

Using one finger, make a small indent in each ball and then fill the hole with half a macadamia or an almond. Seal the dumpling by folding the edge over. Carefully roll it into a ball using the palms of your hands. Set aside.

To make lime syrup, place the sugar, lime juice and zest, and water into a small saucepan over low heat. Stir until sugar has dissolved. Leave it to simmer for around 15 minutes or until it thickens slightly to become a syrup. Strain through a fine sieve and keep warm.

Drop the dumplings into the boiling water and cook for 5–10 minutes. When the dumplings float to the top, leave them in for another 3–5 minutes before removing and placing straight into the syrup. Test one of the dumplings—it should be squishy and cooked right through.

You will need to serve these lovely dumplings immediately after cooking. Peel and deseed mango and slice into pieces. Toast some shredded coconut in a frypan over medium heat for a few minutes until golden. Finely slice a few kaffir lime leaves. Spoon three hot dumplings into each bowl, pour some hot lime syrup over the top and garnish with a few slices of mango, the finely sliced kaffir lime leaves and some shredded coconut. Gorgeous and so simple.

Serve with Gerwurztraminer, Sauvignon Blanc or Muscat.

Spicy Pear Love Cake

Preparation time: 45 minutes

Cooking time: 45 minutes

Gluten-free

A gorgeous gluten-free cake that says simply 'I love you'. Here we see whole spiced-up poached pears studded in a lovely cinnamon and vanilla bean cake. Heavenly served up with our Cinnamon Cream and sprinkled with Praline (see Index).

SPICY SYRUP

350g (12¼oz) caster sugar

300ml (10fl oz) pear juice

1 lemon, juiced and zested

15 cardamom pods, husks removed and seeds
    ground

2 cinnamon quills

6 cloves

¼ teaspoon nutmeg

¼ teaspoon black pepper

1L (36fl oz) water

6 pears, peeled (any small pear such as Corella
    or Beurre Bosc pears are suitable)

CAKE

250g (9oz) butter

150g (5oz) caster sugar

1 teaspoon vanilla paste

6 eggs, separated

150g (5oz) ground almonds

150g (5oz) coarse polenta

1 teaspoon ground cinnamon

½ teaspoon nutmeg

Handful of pecans or walnuts, roughly chopped
    (optional)

SPICY PEAR SYRUP

Combine all syrup ingredients, except the pears, in a saucepan on a medium heat. Bring to the boil and turn the heat down to a simmer.

Squeeze a little lemon juice over the pears to stop them browning. Add the pears to the syrup and

Continues...

cover with a cartouche (cut a circle of baking paper the same size as the saucepan, to make a lid).

Simmer pears for 5 minutes or until slightly tender. Remove pears from the syrup and set aside.

Let the mixture simmer for another hour or until it has reduced to a lovely rich syrup. I like to let it caramelise to a rich amber colour. You may need to add a little more water after caramelising. Strain and set aside.

CAKE

Preheat oven to 180°C (350°F/Gas Mark 4). Grease and line a 20cm (10in) spring-form cake tin.

Cream the butter and sugar until pale. Add the vanilla paste, then the egg yolks, one at a time, and beat. Add the ground almonds, polenta, cinnamon, nutmeg and the nuts (if using).

Whisk egg whites to stiff peaks and fold gently into the cake batter.

Spoon into the greased and lined tin, smooth the top of the batter with a spatula and then press the pears evenly into the cake batter around the cake tin.

Bake on the centre shelf of your oven for 30 minutes. Then reduce the temperature to 160°C (325°F/Gas Mark 2–3), cover the top of the cake with a layer of baking paper and bake for approximately 15 minutes or until this beauty of a cake is firm to touch and a skewer comes out clean.

Once cake is cooked, remove from the oven and prick all over with a skewer. Pour half of the hot syrup over the warm cake and allow to cool.

This cake is hard to resist eating straight away. When ready to enjoy yourself immensely, pour more of the syrup over this divine cake and add a scoop of Crème Fraîche Ice Cream, plain, unsweetened yoghurt with a little honey or your favourite vanilla ice cream. This is gluten-free bliss.

Serve with a glass of Sauternes or Muscat.

ps I love you

Baked Hazelnut Custard with Lime Sugar

Serves 8

Preparation time: 5 minutes

Cooking time: 20 minutes

This recipe is silky smooth, indulgent, full of flavour and so, so easy. You can get creative here too and adjust this recipe to suit your palette. Why not substitute Frangelico for Sambuca, Limoncello for orange liqueur, substitute lime sugar for another citrus or spice—let your imagination run wild.

CUSTARDS

500g (2 cups/15oz) sour cream

395g (13½oz) can sweetened condensed milk

80ml (2½fl oz) Frangelico or your choice of liqueur

LIME SUGAR

1 lime, zested

50g (1¾oz) caster (superfine) sugar

CUSTARD

Preheat oven 180°C (350°F/Gas Mark 4). Whisk all custard ingredients together and place in a jug to suit. Pour evenly into 8 x 125ml (4oz) ramekins. Then place the ramekins in a baking dish filled with water that comes three-quarters of the way up the sides of the ramekins.

Bake in oven for 20 minutes or until firm in the centre. Remove and allow to cool to room temperature. You can also refrigerate until ready to serve. Prepare lime sugar for topping.

LIME SUGAR

Remove the zest of the lime in thin strips, using a vegetable peeler. Make sure to remove any of the bitter white pith from the zest.

Chop the zest and then add the sugar. Grind in a mortar and pestle or food processor until the mixture turns a lime green, leaving a few bits of zest. Sprinkle over each custard and serve. Top with edible flowers—for example, elderflower. If you have no lime, opt for a few crushed hazelnuts...yummo!

ps I love you

Sexy Chocolate Tart

Serves 16
Preparation time: 30 minutes
Cooking time: 40 minutes

There's something ultra sexy about the glossy surface of a chocolate ganache-filled tart. Chocolate, spices, soft buttery pastry—this ultra-rich tart is instant gratification at its finest.
Note: *You can use all dark chocolate or all milk chocolate...whatever tickles your fancy.*

1 quantity Sweet Shortcrust Pastry (see Index)
150g (5oz) dark (semi-sweet) chocolate (I like Lindt 70% cocoa)
150g (5oz) milk chocolate
1½ cups (375ml/13fl oz) pouring cream
8cm (3¼in) knob fresh ginger, finely sliced

10 cardamom pods, crushed in mortar and pestle, seeds removed and ground
3 cinnamon sticks
3 cloves
¼ teaspoon black pepper

Prepare and bake pastry in a 25cm (10in) removable base tart tin.

Place the chocolate in food processor or chop up into small pieces.

Place the cream, ginger slices, ground cardamom, cinnamon sticks, cloves and black pepper in a small saucepan over a medium heat. Bring to the boil, taking it off the heat as soon as it starts to boil. Leave it for the flavours to infuse for half an hour.

Reheat the cream until just boiling again, then strain and pour over the chocolate stirring until smooth and glossy.

Pour the melted chocolate into your tart case and transfer to the refrigerator to set for about 2 hours.

Store the tart in the fridge, but when ready to serve, it is at its best at room temperature. For a welcome playmate, serve with Cinnamon Cream (see Index).

Kids' Party

Remember your favourite childhood party? Bring back simple parties, with sumptuous and fine food for your friends and family.

The Wishing Cake

Serves 8–12

Preparation time: 30 minutes

Cooking time: 40 minutes

This cake it is not only easy to make, it is very versatile. You can make one batch for a modest Sunday chocolate cake munch, or double to make a spectacular birthday cake or dessert. It is a cake for kids and adults alike. Fill and top in with any of the Frosts or Chantilly Cream.

For something extra special try:

Simple Chocolate Ganache with Spiced Cherries, Chocolate-filled Cherries, Berry Frost with Turkish Delight cut up into chunks to reveal its gorgeous pink centre.

Alternatively, for something a little more sophisticated, top with Balsamic Berries or simply Sugared Rose Petals (see Index).

CAKE

250g (9oz) unsalted butter, cubed, soft

300g (10½oz) raw (Demerara) sugar

200g (7oz) dark brown sugar

3 cups (450g/16oz) self-raising (self-rising) flour

4 eggs, beaten

½ cup (4fl oz) hot milk

50g (1¾oz) cocoa

1 teaspoon vanilla extract

100g (3½oz) dark (semisweet) chocolate, grated

2 tablespoons (40g/1½oz) instant coffee of choice

1 cup (250ml/9fl oz) boiling water

Butter and cocoa, for preparing pans (I love to use cocoa instead of flour for dusting cake pans, so that my baked cake comes out with no signs of flour)

FROSTING

100g (3oz) unsalted butter, cubed and softened.

250g (8oz) cream cheese

350 (12oz) icing (confectioners') sugar

150g (5oz) cocoa powder

150g (5oz) sour cream

Continues...

Place all frosting ingredients in a processor and mix until light and fluffy, this should take 3–5 minutes. Set aside.

Preheat oven to 160°C (325°F/Gas Mark 2–3).

Grease and cocoa dust 2 x 20cm (10in) round cake tins.

Using an electric mixer, beat butter and sugars until light and fluffy. Add flour then beaten egg gradually until combined. Do not over mix. Set aside.

Take a small saucepan and warm milk. Then combine milk, cocoa and vanilla in one bowl, and in another add chocolate and coffee to boiling water.

Slowly and alternatively, add these to the flour mix and combine well. Your dough should resemble a mocha-coloured frosting.

Divide batter into the prepared cake tins. Bake for 35–40 minutes or until a bamboo skewer placed in the centre of the cake comes out clean.

When cake is cooked, leave out of oven to cool for 10 minutes, before running a clean butter knife around the edge of the cake and cake pan. Gently turn the cakes out upside down onto desired plates to cool.

I use the base of the cake for the top of cake for frosting, as is a flat and even surface to work with. Top one cake with your choice of frosting or cream, then place the second cake on top and smother it with topping as well. If you want to make a cake tower, slice the cakes horizontally so that you have four cakes and top with frosting and stack as high as you want. Decorate with berries, sweets or something whimsical (see Index).

If you don't want to use round pans here you can use either a 2 x 20cm (10in) square cake tin or any other pan that holds 12 cups (2.8L/94½fl oz). A one-pan option is something you might want to consider if you have impatient little ones keen to get in on all the action at cutting time.

Popsicles

Each recipe makes 12 fun pops

*Why buy store-bought ices when you can make your own simply?
They are far healthier and great for kids playdates, parties or for a
weekend treat. Kids will love these and those adults, who are still
kids on the inside, will adore these too.*

*You can even get the kids involved—they may come up with their own
names and flavours to share proudly with their friends. Remember,
the higher the sugar to water ratio, the less iciness. All will take at least
4 hours to freeze—if you require smaller quantities, just reduce the
recipe. Remember also to choose non-toxic moulds.*

*Get creative—there are so many ways to make these. Use novel ice
block trays and moulds, the humble paper cup and, my favourite, ice
block trays are great. Pop craft sticks, (any craft store) put in upright to
set and viola. Visit your local kitchen shop to look for different shapes
that would make a great pop or choose from an array of popsicles
moulds available—have fun with it. You may like to wait till the ice is
starting to form, for a straight and perfectly centre pop stick.*

Starry Eyes Popsicles

4½ cups (36fl oz) fresh orange juice

1½ cup (12fl oz) fresh carrot juice

Prepare your fresh juice then blend required quantities. Place in desired moulds and freeze for at least 4 hours.

Island Jive Popsicles

1½ cups (12fl oz) coconut cream
¾ cup (180g/6oz) sugar

4½ cups (36fl oz) pineapple juice

Combine coconut cream with sugar. Pour equal quantities of cream mixture into mould and freeze until set. Now remove popsicles from the freezer and pour pineapple juice into mould to make the second layer. Then return to the freezer for at least 4 hours.

Whizzy Fizzy Popsicles

4½ cups (36fl oz) ginger beer

1½ cups (12fl oz) pineapple juice

Prepare fresh juice and combine with ginger beer. Place in moulds, leaving about 1.2cm/½in at top, to allow for expansion, due to the carbonated drink. Yum yum.

Mango Bliss Popsicles

4½ cups (36fl oz) cream
1½ cups (180g/6oz) mango pulp

¾ cup (180g/6oz) sugar (optional)

Combine cream, mango and sugar, then divide evenly into popsicle mould. Place in the freezer for at least 4 hours.

Spider Cider Popsicles

1½ cup (12fl oz) apple and blackcurrant juice

4½ cups (36fl oz) cloudy apple juice

These are great done as striped popsicles, if you have the time. Divide your singular juice quantities by a third. Divide ½ cup of apple and blackcurrant juice equally (as well as you can) into moulds and freeze until set. Remove moulds from freezer, then add 1½ cups of cloudy apple juice divided equally into moulds and freeze. Repeat this layering process three times until all the juice has been used.

Alternatively, just do three-quarter and one-quarter ratio, by taking apple and blackcurrant juice and dividing equally across popsicles, freeze until set. Then add cloudy apple juice to fill popsicle moulds and freeze for at least 4 hours. You can swap this order around to suit your pops.

Berry Magic Popsicles

4½ cup (36fl oz) cream
¾ cup (180g/6oz) sugar

1½ cup (12fl oz) berry coulis (see Index)

In a blender, combine cream and sugar then place in desired moulds. Using a knife, add the berry mix to the moulds and fold it in. This should make a lovely swirling pattern. Then freeze until set, this should take about 4 hours.

Razzle Dazzle Popsicles

These are my daughter's favourite and I'm quite fond of emptying the freezer of them too.

4½ cups (36fl oz) lemonade (cold, flat)

1½ cup (12fl oz) maple syrup

Ginger juice or ground ginger to taste, if desired

In a blender, take lemonade, maple, ginger (if using) and blend. Place in desired moulds and freeze for at least 4 hours.

Honey Bee Popsicles

4½ cup (36 fl oz) apricot nectar

1½ cups (390g/12¼fl oz) plain unsweetened
   yoghurt

¾ cup (180ml/6fl oz) honey

Combine nectar, yoghurt and honey in a blender and then pour into desired popsicle moulds. Freeze for at least 4 hours.

Gummy Gummy Gum Drops

Makes approximately 40

Preparation/Cooking time: 30 minutes

I love the idea of making jubes from scratch for my kids. I was delighted to find an old recipe for the ones I remember delighting in as a child.

2 cups (440g/15oz) caster (superfine) sugar

2 tablespoons (40g/1½oz) gelatine powder

½ cup (125ml/4fl oz) cold water

Natural food colouring

White sugar, for coating

Combine sugar and water in a saucepan over a high heat and boil for 5 minutes. Meanwhile, mix the gelatine powder with ¾ cup (185ml/6fl oz) of cold water. Add the gelatine to the sugar mixture and stir to combine and dissolve. Return to heat and boil slowly for 15 minutes. Stir occasionally. Mixture will foam somewhat.

Remove from heat and place in your desired jube moulds. Refrigerate until set and remove from moulds and roll in white sugar. These are available at most kitchen shops and discount stores. Silicone moulds are best for easy removal.

Skye's Chocolate Avocado Tarts

Serves 4

Preparation time: 40 minutes

Let yourself truly indulge with this silken smooth chocolate mousse with raspberry. Super easy to make, all you need to arm yourself with for this adventure is a blender, a food processor and a spatula. The most important thing to remember is to have fun in the kitchen. Think decadent, think yummy, think wild!

PECAN BASE

140g (5oz) dark (semi-sweet), 70% cocoa, chocolate

3 cups pecan nuts

8 medjool dates

CHOCOLATE AVOCADO MOUSSE

4 large avocadoes

12 tablespoons cacao powder or cocoa

230ml (7¾fl oz) coconut milk

230ml (7¾fl oz) light agave syrup or sugar syrup (see Index)

GARNISH OPTIONS

100g (3½oz) dark (semi-sweet) chocolate, 70% cocoa, shavings or cut into fine slithers

Fresh raspberries, strawberries, orange slices (whatever tickles your fancy and is in season)

BASE

Blitz the chocolate and ½ cup of the pecans in the food processor until you have small chunks. Set aside in a bowl.

Take the pits out of the dates and throw into the food processor along with 1 cup of pecans. Process until you have fine crumbs and the mixture presses together easily.

Mix the chocolate and pecan pieces with the crumbs.

Scoop about 2 tablespoons of the crust into around 8 x 8cm (3¼in) bottomless tart tins. Using your fingertips, firmly press the crust into the tart tin, leaving a cavity in the centre to hold the cream. Place in the freezer to set.

Continues...

CHOCOLATE AVOCADO MOUSSE

Combine avocadoes, cacao, coconut milk, agave syrup (or honey or sugar syrup), in a blender until smooth and creamy. Taste and adjust if need be, as produce is always very different. With the cacao, varying brands are quite different in their strength. Start with 8 tablespoons and then taste to see if it needs more. If you want your mousse to be sweeter, add more agave nectar. Less sweet and less chocolaty, more avocado. More chocolaty, add more cacao powder.

TO SERVE

Grab your tart cases out of the freezer. Spoon a couple of tablespoons of your chocolate avocado mousse into each tart case and swirl with the back of a teaspoon.

Sprinkle your dark chocolate shavings on top of your magnificent mousse and place in freezer until the desserts are semi-frozen. When you are ready to serve, just throw your fresh fruit on top and you're good to go! If you make ahead of time, pull out of the freezer around 30 minutes before serving. You can also just place the tarts in the fridge before serving. They are lovely cold or semi-frozen.

Mini Ice Cream Sandwiches

Serves 12 (24 cookies to make 12 sandwiches)

Preparation time: 10 minutes

Cooking time: 6 minutes

If you have a theme for your party, consider the colour choice of the toppings for maximum impact and pizzazz. You can make this job an activity as part of your party plan if you think they (and you) are up for it!

125g (4oz) butter

1 cup (150g/5oz) brown sugar

1 large egg

1 teaspoon vanilla essence or vanilla bean paste

1¾ cups (270g/9½oz) self-raising
    (self-rising) flour

1 cup milk chocolate chips

1 x 500ml (17½fl oz) tub of vanilla ice cream

DECORATION

Place 1 cup of any or all of the following into
    separate bowls for decorating fun!

Chocolate chips, milk or white

Mini marshmallows

Chocolate sprinkles (any sprinkles)

Smarties

Mini jellybeans

Crushed honeycomb

Or your child's favourite sweet, the options are
    limitless.

Preheat oven to 160°C (325°F/Gas Mark 2–3).

To make chewy chocolate chip cookies, melt butter in saucepan over medium heat and set aside to cool a little. Pour butter into a large bowl, stir in sugar, mix until smooth and sugar is mainly dissolved.

Beat the egg with a whisk or fork, add vanilla and stir into the sugar mixture. Set aside.

Sift flours into a small bowl and gradually mix into the sugar mixture until combined.

Continues...

Stir through the chocolate chips.

To form the cookies, scoop a tablespoon of the cookie mixture into the palm of your hand and roll into a ball.

Place cookie balls about 5cm (2in) apart onto lined baking trays to allow them to spread.

Press down on top of the balls a little.

Bake for approximately 6 minutes or until almost golden. You want them to be slightly chewy. Then remove from oven and allow to cool on trays for 3 minutes before transferring to a wire rack to cool completely.

Once cookies are cool, take one cookie, place upside down and scoop ice cream on top. Then place another cookie right side up to make a sandwich and gently squish together.

Choose from your range of embellishments and roll the exposed ice cream on sides of sandwiches through the sweets.

Serve immediately.

Fruit Skewers

Makes 24

Preparation time: 10–15 minutes

These look spectacular and kiddies love 'em. What's more they couldn't be easier. Serve alone or pop a few of them on the top of a cake for impact and splashes of colour.

Kiwi Skewers

6 kiwi fruit, firm   24 bamboo skewers

Peel the skin carefully off fruit trying to keep the shape intact. Cut each kiwi fruit across-ways into 4 thick slices. Take your bamboo skewers and cut off sharp ends for safety. Insert a skewer into the side of each kiwi fruit slice.

Marshmallow, Raspberry and Strawberry Skewers

Try mixing healthy fruit skewers with a few treats like fluffy marshmallows. These will bring smiles to little faces. Allow at least three of each ingredient on every skewer. The amounts you buy will depend on how many mouths you are feeding.

Marshmallows (pink and white)   Fresh strawberries
Fresh raspberries   Bamboo skewers

Take your bamboo skewers and cut off sharp ends for safety.
    Place a marshmallow, raspberry and strawberry on the skewer and repeat.
    Sweet and simple!

Tough Times Can Be Sweet

Hold on to your purse strings peeps. This is an utterly delicious collection for frugal times—living better for less.

Passionfruit Granita

Serves 4

Preparation time: 30 minutes

Passionfruit is a fruit of my childhood—it grew like crazy in every backyard I knew.
Light and refreshing, this dessert will delight young and old. You can also use bought passionfruit pulp with
success and, if needed, omit the mascarpone for a dairy-free and even more cost-effective option.

2 ¼ cups (375 ml/13oz) filtered water

1⅓ cups (400g/13oz) sugar

1½ cup passionfruit pulp (275ml/10fl oz) or about
16 passionfruits (if you aren't a fan of seeds,
strain the pulp before using)

200g (7fl oz) mascarpone

2 tablespoons (10ml) lemon juice

Pinch of salt

White chocolate curls (optional)

In a heavy-based saucepan, combine water and sugar. Bring to boil over high heat, stirring until sugar dissolves, then turn off heat. In a large mixing bowl place passionfruit, mascarpone, lemon juice and salt and fold together until well combined. Take a small sieve and remove passionfruit seeds if desired.

Add the sugar syrup to fruit mixture and stir (do not use a blender, if you want to keep the seeds).

Leave to cool completely, this should take about 20 minutes.

Then place mixture in an airtight container and freeze for 4 hours, stirring and scraping with a fork every 20 minutes. Even out crystals when and where necessary. Place on bottom of freezer for best results and consume within 24 hours.

Serve in glass bowls or glassware, top with a curl of white chocolate.

If using an ice cream machine, just follow your manufacturer's instructions.

Coffee Granita

Serves 4

Coffee granita is spectacular. It makes a lovely addition to any dinner party menu. It's easy and because you choose the coffee, the flavour options are limitless. The ingredients are minimal and inexpensive.

2 cups (500ml/16fl oz) freshly brewed espresso coffee (or instant if you like)
½ cup (110g/12oz) caster (superfine) sugar
1 teaspoon lemon zest

Mint sprigs, to garnish
Whipped cream, to serve
Coffee liqueur, to serve

In a large mixing bowl, whisk together coffee, sugar and zest until the sugar dissolves.

Place in an airtight container and freeze for 3 hours, stirring with a fork every 20 minutes. Even out crystals when and where necessary.

If you cannot allow the time to nurse your granita, place your mix into 2 or 3 ice trays, freeze for 3 hours, then remove from tray and process in a blender. The result will be a little watery.

Serve in glass bowls or glasses, top with a sprig of mint or a dollop of whipped cream for a Sicilian-style treat or drizzle with a little coffee liqueur, if desired.

tough times can be sweet

Elderflower Jelly with Fruit

Serves 4 (fits a 600ml/21fl oz jelly mould)
Preparation time: 10 minutes

Elderflower is a beautiful aromatic herb known for its floral heads of miniature white, lacy blooms that conjure up rolling hillsides and country picnics. It has a floral and grapey flavour and the cordial makes a terrific drink in summer. Enjoy this magnificent and transparent jelly served in a large jelly mould or prepare in a tray to set, and then cut into tiny cubes to dress a dessert. Delicate, light, aromatic and refreshing, the cordial makes a terrific addition to sparkling mineral water or champagne. Try poured over Crème Fraîche Ice cream or Champagne Sorbet (see Index) for summer delight!

Note: *Jelly does not like heat, so don't serve up on a buffet table in summer.*

250ml (1 cup/8fl oz) elderflower cordial
350ml 11½fl oz) filtered water
6 gelatine leaves

100g green grapes, halved (optional)
(You can also use berries or apples, cored, halved and finely sliced.)

In a jug or large bowl combine cordial and water. Set aside.

Soak gelatine leaves in just enough water to cover them and leave for about 5 minutes.

In a medium saucepan add cordial and warm, do not boil.

Squeeze excess water from gelatine leaves. Stir the gelatine into the cordial mix and mix until gelatine dissolves. Add fruit here, if you like, then pour mixture into desired moulds. Refrigerate overnight to set.

When I am making this to cut into small cubes for a bit of bling, I pour the mixture into a shallow dish to set. Then I cut pieces into 1cm (⅓in) cubes, sometimes smaller.

French Brûlée Toast

Serves 6

Super easy! A lovely choice for breakfast or brunch, to make for one or more. I love to make this on Sundays or for my sleepover guests. Sometimes I pair it with yoghurt and extra maple syrup or a rasher of bacon.
Note: *The better the bread, the better the outcome, so visit your local baker. I like to use gluten-free white available at leading supermarkets, due to its milk content, or challah bread—yummo!*

2 eggs plus 2 extra yolks

1 cup (125 ml/4 ½ fl oz) thickened cream

125ml (4oz) maple syrup

1 teaspoon vanilla paste or extract

Butter, for frying

1 loaf of bread, baguette, sliced on the bias (spunkier that way), stale is okay

3 tablespoons sugar

Maple syrup or honey, for drizzling on each serve

Icing (confectioners') sugar, for dusting

In a medium-sized mixing bowl, whisk eggs, cream, maple syrup and vanilla until fluffy. Set aside.

Place your frypan on a medium heat and add butter.

Dip your sliced bread into the custard mix, soaking both sides. Lay the slice in the frypan and cook each side for about 2 minutes until golden brown.

Remove from pan and coat one side of each slice with sugar and either pop under the grill on a medium heat or blow torch the toast till the sugar caramelises. Serve on plates with a generous drizzle of maple syrup or honey and dust with icing sugar.

For a drop-dead gorgeous version, add Roasted Peaches (see Index).

Espresso Cookies

Makes 24
Preparation time: 15 minutes
Cooking time: 20 minutes

Espresso cookies are delightful. A soft sweetly spiced, buttery biscuit, these are great served alongside a decadent Coffee Crème Pot (see Index), for all of you coffee fiends out there.

½ cup (125g/4oz) unsalted butter or dairy-free margarine

½ cup (75g/2½oz) brown sugar

2 tablespoons (40ml/1½fl oz) treacle

½ tablespoon (10g) freshly made espresso coffee

½ tablespoon (10g) ground espresso beans

½ teaspoon vanilla extract

1½ cups (225g/8oz) gluten-free plain (all-purpose) flour

Espresso beans, to garnish

Preheat oven to 130°C (275°F/Gas Mark 1).

In a large mixing bowl, beat together butter and sugar. Add treacle, coffee, beans and vanilla. Add flour next and combine well. Lightly grease a baking tray. Roll dough into balls and place on baking tray. Lightly flatten with a fork and place a single espresso bean in the centre of each one. Bake for 20–25 minutes, remove from oven and leave to cool.

Store in an airtight container.

Coffee Crème Pots

Serves 6
Preparation time: 20 minutes
Cooking time: 30 minutes

Love coffee? You will love a coffee crème pot. They are fit for any special occasion and will impress morning, noon or night.

3 cups (750ml/24fl oz) cream
½ cup (3½oz) ground coffee
5 large egg yolks (at room temperature)
½ cup (110g/3½oz) sugar

30ml (6 teaspoons/1fl oz) coffee liqueur (optional)
Additional whipped cream for garnish, if desired
6 coffee beans

Preheat oven 160°C (325°F/Gas Mark 2-3)

In a medium saucepan, combine cream and ground coffee and bring to just under boil on a medium heat. Remove from heat then pour through a fine sieve to remove all the grounds. You must do this otherwise you end up with a gritty texture to your pots. Cover and set aside.

In a bowl, whisk the egg yolks and sugar. Set aside. Add the liqueur to the hot coffee mixture here if using. Slowly mix the hot coffee mixture into the yolks until blended. Pour mixture into a jug and evenly divide liquid into 6 crème pots. If you want to bake in a cup like the one picture, make sure it is an ovenproof one.

Place pots in a baking dish filled with water that comes three-quarters of the way up the sides of the pots. Cover the tray lightly with aluminium foil and bake for 30 minutes. Cool completely and top with a dollop of whipped cream or Cinnamon Cream (see Index) and a single coffee bean.

Easy Peasy

Life and food doesn't have to be complicated. Here's a bunch of easy recipes—just pure and simple, delectable desserts. The produce takes centre stage, no fluffing and flouncing about.

Uncle Bruce's Extravaganza with Summer Berries

Serves 4

Preparation/Cooking time: 15 minutes

If you were lucky enough to be invited for dinner, Uncle Bruce always cooked only two meals, with great expertise—roast lamb made on his '25-year-old lard' (dripping from roasts gone by) and the other dish was his famous dessert, Extravaganza with Berries. His simple but super delicious dessert would make the whole table fall silent as we devoured this sweet sensation. I asked Uncle Bruce what was in it and was pleasantly surprised by the simplicity of this brilliant recipe. Truly, it just doesn't get any simpler. Thank you Uncle Bruce. Please don't disown me as I share our family secret.

Note: *If the berries are too expensive or not in season, you can use any fruit you like, or leave the prosecco and icing sugar off and just serve fruit with the extravaganza cream.*

1 punnet raspberries, washed

1 punnet blueberries, washed

1 punnet strawberries, washed, tops cut off and quartered

1 cup Prosecco (sparkling Italian wine) or any fruity sparkling wine (leave out if you don't like sparkling wine)

2 tablespoons icing (confectioners') sugar

Small handful of pistachio, macadamia or another nut you love, lightly chopped

EXTRAVAGANZA CREAM

250g (8¾oz) crème fraîche or sour cream

2 tablespoons (35g/1¼oz) brown sugar

Place the berries in a bowl, pour the prosecco and icing sugar over them and set aside to macerate.

Lightly toast the nuts in a frypan over a low-medium heat for approximately 5 minutes or until lightly golden brown.

To make the Extravaganza Cream, whisk the crème fraîche with the sugar in a bowl until combined.

Place the macerated berries and a little of the liquid equally in each of the glasses to serve. Put aside the Prosecco liquid for drinking. Dollop the cream on top of the berries and garnish with the nuts.

easy peasy

Nectarine and Honey Ice Cream

Serves 4

Preparation/Cooking time: 5 minutes

I highly recommend sharing this with your family and friends. This nectarine goodness is certain to keep everyone happy. Nectarine and honey are a match made in heaven, high in vitamin C, this sweet will leave you feeling incredibly refreshed. You can also try other fruit such as mango, pineapple, mulberries or bananas.

6 nectarines

2 tablespoons local honey

Handful of mint or baby basil leaves

Take fresh, raw, ripe nectarines. Peel, deseed and slice then store slices in plastic bag or other suitable container and freeze.

When you are ready to make this dessert, remove from freezer and allow nectarines to partially thaw. The nectarines should not fully thaw: they should still have ice crystals in them.

Put partially thawed nectarines and honey in blender and puree. Serve in a beautiful glass and garnish with mint or basil leaves.

Freeform Apple Crumble

Serves 4

Cooking time: 30 minutes

This is the classic apple crumble on the run. Quick, dead easy and oh-so-tasty. Not quite as light as a regular apple crumble, but so much faster and easier to make.

2 tablespoons butter

3 Jazz, Braeburn or Granny Smith apples, peeled, quartered and sliced

2 tablespoons brown sugar

2 cups rolled oats

¾ cup milk powder

1 teaspoon nutmeg

Pinch of ground cinnamon

½ teaspoon vanilla paste

Handful of pecans or walnuts (lightly chopped)

100g (3½oz) butter

½ cup honey

1 tablespoon shredded coconut, sprinkled on top (optional)

CREAM

150ml (5fl oz) crème fraîche or sour cream

150ml (5fl oz) natural yoghurt

1½ tablespoons brown sugar

Melt the butter in a frying pan over medium heat until foaming. Add apple and cook for approximately 10 minutes or until golden. Add brown sugar and cook, stirring, for 5 minutes or until apple is tender and you have a yummy caramel.

To make crumble, combine remaining dry ingredients and set aside. Place butter and honey in an oven-safe frypan and warm until butter is melted. Pour butter mixture into the dry ingredients and combine. Grab 4 individual pudding dishes or vessels. Place spoonfuls of the caramelised apples and crumble into your pudding basins. Sprinkle coconut on top, if using. Place your dishes under grill until browned on top (about 5 minutes).

To make the cream, whisk the crème fraîche with the yoghurt and sugar in a bowl until combined.

To serve, dollop cream or ice cream on top. Feel free to sprinkle a smidgen of cinnamon on top of the cream.

Roasted Peaches
with Orange Blossom Yoghurt

Serves 4
Preparation time: 15 minutes
Cooking time: 25 minutes

Peaches, mmm, I love peaches. I prefer white peaches but use either for this recipe. Serve with lashings of Orange Blossom Yoghurt or Vanilla Cream (see Index) and savour every mouthful. If you want to feed a crowd, adjust the recipe accordingly. It's a sensational addition to French Brûlée Toast (see Index).

Butter, for greasing
250g (8¾oz) plain, unsweetened yoghurt
2 tablespoons honey
¹⁄₈ teaspoon orange blossom water (if you can't find this, just leave it out)

4 peaches, halved and deseeded
1 tablespoons raw (demerara) sugar
2 teaspoons vanilla paste

Preheat oven to 180°C (350°F/Gas Mark 4). Grease a roasting pan or cake tin with butter. Combine the yoghurt, honey and orange blossom water and set aside.

In a small bowl, toss peaches in sugar and vanilla paste and place in the baking tray. Bake for 25 minutes.

Serve this scrumptious dessert with the orange blossom yoghurt, whipped or double cream.

Off the Wagon

Here's a sweet collection for when you need a little comfort—you're off the wagon,
you've broken up with your partner, perhaps you missed out on a job, or you're just
singing the blues. Together we can get through it, one ice cream sandwich at a time.
They're only sweets, we know. But small things can make a big difference.

Chocoholics Anonymous Ice Cream Sandwich

Serves 8

Preparation time: 20 minutes

Cooking time: 8 minutes per tray

For moments when only chocolate will do, this ice cream sandwich is most certainly the way forward. If you're up for some nurturing baking, these cookies have a hit of cranberries, which are tart and balance all of the rich chocolate. Make these yummy cookies and sandwich chocolate ice cream for the ultimate chocaholics experience.

COOKIES

125g (4oz) butter

1 cup (160g/5oz) brown sugar

1 large egg

1 teaspoon vanilla essence

1¾ cups (190g/6¼oz) self-raising (self-rising) flour

1 cup (190g/6oz) dark (semi-sweet),

70% cocoa, chocolate cut up into chunks

Handful of dried cranberries

1 x 500ml tub of chocolate ice cream or 1 quantity of Crème Fraîche Ice Cream and mix in 3 tablespoons of cocoa powder for chocolatey goodness

3 tablespoons cocoa powder

Berry coulis (optional)

Preheat the oven to 160°C (325°F/Gas Mark 2–3). Line two baking trays with baking paper.

Melt butter in a saucepan over medium heat and set aside to cool a little.

Pour butter into a large bowl, stir in brown sugar until smooth and sugar is mainly dissolved.

Beat the egg and vanilla with a whisk or fork to combine and stir into the sugar mixture. Sift flour into a small bowl and gradually mix into sugar and egg mixture until combined. Stir through chocolate chips and cranberries.

Continues...

To form the cookies, scoop a teaspoon of the cookie mixture into the palm of your hands and roll it into a ball. Place cookie balls about 5cm (2in) apart onto lined baking trays. Press down on the top of the balls a little.

Bake for 6 minutes or until just golden then remove from oven and allow to cool on trays for 3 minutes before transferring to a wire rack to cool completely.

To assemble, once cookies are cool, spoon loads of chocolate ice cream in between two of your luscious choc chip cookies. Feel free to add a splash of berry coulis (see Index) between the cookies to turn this sucker into a giant Monte Carlo. Squish it together, use a butter knife or a pallet knife and tidy the edges, and serve straight away. This indulgent treat is fit for serious lounging.

For complete slothism, simply buy some chewy chocolate cookies and sandwich your favourite chocolate ice cream in between.

Capitol

RECORDS

"Tomorrow's Hits

Parlophone
MADE IN ENGLAND

R. 3118

COUNT YOUR BLESSINGS
(Temple—Morgan)
THE LUTON GIRLS CHOIR
With Orchestra
Conducted by George Melachrino

NCB

Crème Brûlée, to end all Crème Brûlées

Serves 6

Downright decadent, it is no wonder crème brûlée is so popular. Be attentive with this and you will be delighted with the results, as will the smiling recipients you share this with.

4 egg yolks
80g (2½oz) caster (superfine) sugar
300ml (10¼fl oz/1¼ cup) cream
300ml (10¼fl oz/1¼ cup) thickened cream

1 teaspoon (5ml) vanilla extract
30g (6 teaspoon/1oz) icing sugar, to caramelise
    on top of brûlée

Preheat oven 160°C (325°F/Gas Mark 2–3).

Prepare 6 x 125ml (4fl oz) ramekins, by placing them in a baking tray, spread out evenly and filling the baking tray with boiling water, three-quarters of the way up the sides of the ramekins.

In a medium mixing bowl, cream egg yolks and sugar. Set aside.

In a medium, heavy-based saucepan, whisk creams together and add vanilla. When combined, bring to just under the boil over a heat, where little bubbles start to surface.

Take of the heat, pour a small amount of the cream into the egg mixture, and whisk well then add the rest of the cream slowly while still whisking.

Return the mixture to the stove in a saucepan over low heat and mix continuously with a wooden spoon.

To test if the crème is ready, dip your spoon into the mixture and run your finger over the back of the spoon, making a clean wipe. If the custard runs over it requires more time. If it remains in place and doesn't run over your wipe, it is ready.

Continues...

Transfer the custard to a pouring jug and divide into the six prepared ramekins and place on the middle shelf of your oven. Be prepared here, as you want to transfer the mixture immediately to the oven so you don't end up with scrambled eggs for dessert.

Bake for 20–25 minutes. It is ready when it feels just set in the middle of the brûlée.

Carefully remove from the oven and baking tray and leave to cool to room temperature; this should take about 30 minutes.

Then place in the fridge for at least 2 hours before removing to serve.

To serve, sprinkle each brûlée with icing sugar. It is best to use a shaker or fine sieve here to avoid lumps of sugar and give an even covering.

Either place the brûlée under a grill, or use a blowtorch to caramelise the top, until it starts to brown and bubble.

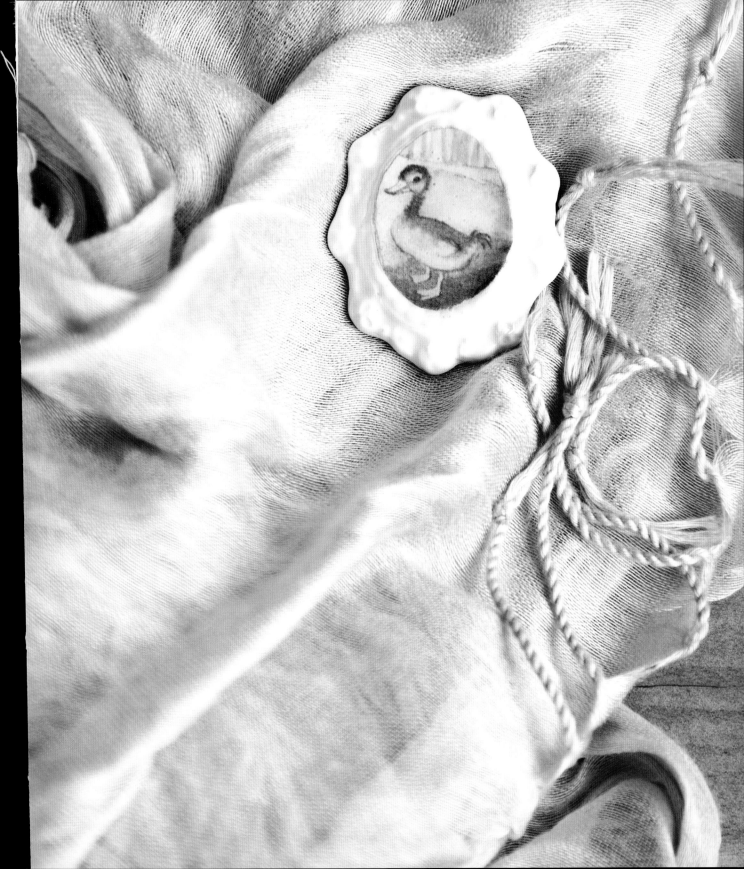

Elvis Presley Parfait

Serves 1 (but Elvis will be happy to share I'm sure)

According to various reports, Elvis Presley's favourite sandwich was peanut butter, caramelised bananas and bacon. He has been described as talking 'feverishly until dawn' while wolfing down the sandwiches. Although we have omitted the bacon, The King himself would have loved this delectable treat packed full of his favourite ammunition. The King and I are sharing this treat.

1 cup of vanilla ice cream

2-3 tablespoons plain, unsweetened yoghurt

2 tablespoons crunchy peanut butter

2 bananas, peeled and cut lengthways or 1 quantity of Brazilian Caramelised Bananas (see Index)

GARNISH

Handful of blueberries (optional)

Small handful of chocolate chunks (I like dark chocolate) or one quantity of Chocolate Ganache (see Index)

Combine your vanilla ice cream of choice with the yoghurt and peanut butter. Throw your banana pieces or Brazilian caramelised bananas beside it. Garnish with blueberries, chocolate chunks of choice or chocolate ganache sauce to drown your bananas in.

Orange and Nutmeg Pudding

Preparation time: 15 minutes

Cooking time: 40 minutes

Who doesn't love a good pud as a winter warmer? This scrumptious pudding is a culmination of our gorgeous friend Helen's delightful bread and butter pud, the exceptionally good croissant-based pud from my lifelong friends Melanie Starr-Ingersol and Jared Ingersol and my own little tweaks.

4 large croissants, cut in half (or 8 small croissants, cut in half)

150g (4½oz) white chocolate, chopped into chunks

50g (1¾oz) dark chocolate, chopped into chunks

Handful of pecan nuts

350ml (12oz) pouring cream

80ml (2½fl oz) double cream

4 large eggs

180g (6oz) caster (superfine) sugar

½ orange, juiced and rind grated finely

¼ teaspoon nutmeg, freshly grated

Preheat oven to 180ºC (350ºF/Gas Mark 4). Grease a large baking dish.

Cover dish with one layer of croissants, sprinkle in the chocolate, nuts then cover with another layer of croissants.

Mix cream together, then whisk in the eggs, sugar, orange juice and rind and pour over croissants in dish.

Grate nutmeg on top and bake for 30–40 minutes. Serve warm with Cinnamon Cream, Chantilly Cream or Crème Fraîche Ice Cream (see Index).

Health Nut

If you're anything like us dessert maniacs, you may feel compelled to eat sweets every day. We have created these healthier desserts, so you can take care of your body, while taking care of your tastebuds.

Caffeine Amigo Cashew Ice Cream

Serves 8

Gluten-free, dairy-free

What a deceptive little Amigo this dessert is. For a dairy-free and gluten-free number, this is surprisingly rich, decadent and, flavour-wise, really packs a punch—just the way I like it. Dessert-making really doesn't get any easier. This is wonderful for a dinner party, as you can make them up to one week before and you can just bust them out of the freezer to be served semi-frozen.

Note: *You can roast hazelnuts quite easily, by placing them on a tray and popping them into a preheated oven at 180°C (350°F) for approximately 10–15 minutes or until skins start to become wrinkly and fall away easily. You can remove the skins by placing them in a tea towel and rubbing them together.*

100ml (3¼fl oz) fresh percolated coffee or 4 teaspoons instant coffee with 100ml (3¼fl oz) of hot water

1 cup raw unsalted cashews

80g (2¾ oz) cacao powder or cocoa

¾ cups agave syrup, honey or maple syrup

1 cup coconut milk

Handful of hazelnuts, roasted (if you have the time), chopped into small chunks (see Note)

Let coffee cool for 5 minutes. Blend all ingredients except hazelnuts in a high-powered blender until the cashew cream is smooth and silky. If there is still a grain in the cream, strain the mixture through a fine sieve.

Spoon into beautiful glasses, sprinkle with roasted hazelnuts, place in freezer for a few hours and then devour. You can make these ahead of time, just place in an airtight container and pull out of the freezer 45 minutes before serving.

Mint Chocolate Tart

Serves 10–12

Preparation time: 30 minutes

I first made this a few Christmases ago, to cater for my beloved in-laws, Barrie and Isla. They had decided to make a lifestyle change for their health and wellbeing and their regime was strict. While they were so incredibly disciplined (something to admire) I knew that they would appreciate a little sweetie to join in the festivities. So I made this treat, which proved a winner with everyone else too. Right then, I feel in love with raw desserts.

BASE

3 cups (750g/26½oz) pecan nuts

3 tablespoons (60ml/2fl oz) coconut oil, melted

150g (5oz) finely chopped dark chocolate

Pinch of salt

FILLING

3½ cup (450g) raw cashews, soaked overnight

2 cups fresh mint, packed (stalks removed)

120g (4oz) refined coconut oil, melted

50g (1¾oz) raw cacao butter

2 teaspoons (10ml) vanilla

100g (2½oz) raw (Demerara) sugar

2–3 drops mint essential oil

Chocolate shavings, to garnish (optional)

BASE

Process all the ingredients, until they resemble a fine crumb (do not mix).

Spread and press mixture into the base and sides of a 34 x 11cm (13 x 4in) rectangular tart tin with removable base. Place in the freezer while you are preparing the filling.

FILLING

Combine all ingredients in a blender or processor and pour into the prepared tart tin.

Place in fridge to set. This dessert can be prepared days ahead and frozen until required.

Let sit at room temperature for 10 minutes or so before cutting with a sharp knife.

Tangelo and Orange Blossom Cashew Ice Cream

Serves 6

Preparation/Cooking time: 30 minutes

Gluten-free, dairy-free

The tangelo, one of my favourite citrus fruits, is a hybrid of a tangerine and either a pomelo or a grapefruit. This dessert is rich, tangy, vibrant and a great treat for lactose or gluten intolerant people.

1 cup cashews, raw unsalted

¾ cup tangelo juice, freshly squeezed

2 tablespoons agave syrup, honey or maple syrup

2 tablespoons refined coconut oil (fragrance free)

¼ cup coconut milk

¼ teaspoon orange blossom essence (optional)

¼ cup macadamia or brazil nuts, raw, unsalted

Blend all ingredients except for the nuts in a high-powered blender until the cashew cream is smooth and silky. If the mixture is not 100% smooth, then strain through a fine sieve. If you have an ice cream machine, then churn this mix before moving onto the next step. If you don't have an ice cream machine, no problem, just move onto the next step.

Place a few macadamias in the bottom of some beautiful glasses then pour orange blossom mix over the top, and place in freezer for at least 3 hours to freeze.

You can store these gorgeous treats for up to one month in a sealed container in your freezer. They are best served semi-frozen, so take them out of the freezer to partially thaw for approximately half an hour before serving.

Lemon and Raspberry Semifreddo

Serves 8

Preparation time: 20 minutes

Freezing time: overnight

Gluten-free, dairy-free (if not using the ice cream)

You can easily make this lovely lemony dessert days before a dinner party. When you're ready to serve, just pull together all of the components. Lemon and raspberry truly are a joyous match.

3 cups cashews, raw unsalted

½ cup honey, agave syrup or sugar syrup

2½ cups coconut milk

1¼ cups lemon juice, and rind finely grated (or add 3 drops lemon myrtle oil)

Pinch of salt

Handful of fresh or frozen raspberries

Handful of macadamia or Brazil nuts, raw unsalted, roughly chopped

Edible flowers (local to your area) (optional)

Shavings of Crème Fraîche Ice Cream (see Index) (optional)

Blend cashews, honey, coconut milk, juice and salt in a high-powered blender until cashews have turned into a smooth cream. If there is still a grain in the cream, strain the mixture through a fine sieve.

Carefully fold your raspberries and nuts through the lemon cream and then pour into a nut roll tin (see Handy Tips). Wrap aluminium foil on each end of the tin. Place in the freezer overnight.

When ready to serve, warm the outside of the nut roll tin with your hands or dip in some hot water for a few seconds. Take a hot knife, cut a slice of the log and place on a plate. To dress it up, scatter a few edible flowers on the plate and put a few shavings on the dessert or add some Berry Coulis (see Index).

Easy version: Place a few nuts and a few raspberries into eight beautiful glasses. Make your cashew cream, fold in your raspberries and pour into your glasses. Place in freezer for at least 4 hours and you are ready to serve. Pull out of the freezer 30 minutes before serving and serve semi-frozen.

Garnish with a few fresh raspberries or edible flowers.

Mango Coconut Creams

Serves 8

Preparation time: 25 minutes

Gluten-free, dairy-free

It really is hard to pick that there is no dairy in this dessert, as it is lovely and creamy. Best served semi-frozen and will keep in the freezer for weeks.

BASE
1 cup pecan nuts
1 cup macadamia or Brazil nuts
7 medjool dates

MANGO COCONUT CREAMS
170g mango (6oz), just over half of one mango, seed removed and chopped up

½ cup cashews, raw, unsalted
3 tablespoons honey, agave, maple or sugar syrup
⅔ cup coconut milk
1½ tablespoons lime juice
⅓ cup coconut oil or butter (optional)

GARNISH
1 fresh mango or 1 kiwi fruit, sliced

BASE
Pit the dates and throw into the food processor along with your nuts. Process until you have fine crumbs and the mixture presses together easily. Scoop about 2 tablespoons of the crust into 6 x 10cm (4in) rectangular bottomless tart tins and press the crust into the tart base. Place in the freezer to set.

MANGO COCONUT CREAMS
Blend the ingredients for the Creams in a food processor until smooth and creamy. If your coconut oil is solid, heat slightly till liquid again. Strain through a fine sieve to make it extra silky smooth. Grab tart cases out of the freezer, pour your mango cream, filling to the top of your tart tin. Place in the freezer for at least 4 hours.

Make these days before a dinner party, place in an airtight container and when you are ready to serve, pull out of freezer 45 minutes before garnishing with your mango or kiwi slices.

Pink Grapefruit and Pomegranate Salad

Serves 4

Preparation time: 10 minutes

This is a delightfully light and beautifully tasting dessert salad. Share with friends in the warm winter sun, with a glass of bubbly. Divine.

4 pink grapefruits

Seeds of 1 pomegranate

½ cup (125ml/4fl oz) orange juice, freshly squeezed

Peel and segment the pink grapefruits and place in a large bowl. Remove the seeds from the pomegranate and add to the grapefruit. Pour over the prepared orange juice and refrigerate for 30 minutes, before serving. Serve with Orange Mascarpone, if desired.

Orange Mascarpone

250g (8oz/1 cup) mascarpone

2 teaspoons orange zest

1 tablespoon (20ml/1fl oz) orange juice

1 teaspoon raw sugar

Combine all ingredients well in a small bowl. Place a dollop of the mascarpone cream on top of salad before serving.

Coconut and Lime Bombe

Preparation time: 45 minutes

Freezing time: 8 hours

Gluten-free, dairy-free

One of Wild Sugar's first desserts to hit the streets, a simpler version of the coconut lime bombe became an instant favourite of our customers when we opened up our tiny market stall very early one Sunday morning.

Note: *If your coconut oil has solidified, warm the container of oil by placing it in a bowl of hot water.*

LIME CREAM
4 limes, juiced

1 cup (250ml/9fl oz) agave or sugar syrup
(see Index)

3 cups avocado, mashed

Pinch of salt

½ cup coconut oil

COCONUT CREAM
1 cup cashews, raw and unsalted

3 tablespoons agave or sugar syrup (see Index)

Pinch of salt

1½ cups coconut cream

1 lemon, juiced

¼ cup coconut oil

Handful of macadamia or Brazil nuts, roughly
chopped

GARNISH
White edible flower petals (we used gardenia
petals), dessicated coconut or coconut flakes

LIME CREAM
Combine all lime cream ingredients in a high-powered food processor and blend till your heart's content. The filling should be smooth and creamy. No chunks my friends, no chunks.

Continues...

Taste and adjust as produce is always very different. If you want your filling to be more sweet, add more agave syrup. Less sweet, more avocado. More acidic, add lime juice, less acidic, more avocado.

Pour the lime cream into a small, deep bowl (it will need to be smaller than the 20cm (8in) bowl or bombe mould you use for the coconut cream). Tap it on the bench to even out the layer and remove air bubbles. Place in the freezer for at least 4 hours until set.

COCONUT CREAM

Blend cashews, agave syrup, coconut cream, lemon juice and coconut oil in a high-powered food processor or blender until cashews have turned into a smooth cream. If there is still a grain in the cream, strain the mixture through a fine sieve and set aside.

BOMBE

Remove the lime cream from the freeze and place in a bowl of hot water for 5 seconds. Using a palette knife, carefully scrape around the edges of the bowl to remove the lime cream from its mould. Remove cling film from the frozen lime cream.

Line a 20cm (8in) pudding basin or dolly varden mould with 2 layers of cling film. Pour half of the coconut cream into a bombe mould that is larger than your lime cream mould (approximately 20cm (8in) in diameter). Place your frozen lime cream in the middle of the bigger mould, then pour the rest of the coconut cream around the frozen lime cream and place in the freezer for another 8 hours to set.

TO SERVE

Remove your bombe from the freezer. Carefully remove the frozen dessert from its mould by running a hot cloth over the pudding basin and using a pallet knife around the edges.

Place it on a plate or pretty pedestal. Grab your edible flower petals, dessicated coconut or coconut flakes and press them into all sides of the bombe. This sweet treat is worth the wait.

Quick Pineapple and Mint Sorbet

Serves 4

Preparation/Cooking time: 5 minutes

Absolutely scrumptious, low fat and very very simple. Grab yourself a lovely fresh pineapple. You can tell if it's ripe by simply pulling at one of the inner leaves. If it comes out easily, your pineapple is ready to go. You can whip this beauty up in 2 minutes.

1 ripe pineapple, skin and core removed, cut up
    into pieces and frozen
Handful of fresh mint

Honey, to drizzle

Partially thaw the pineapples then place them in a blender or food processor along with the mint and honey and puree.

Serve in a beautiful glass and garnish with mint leaves.

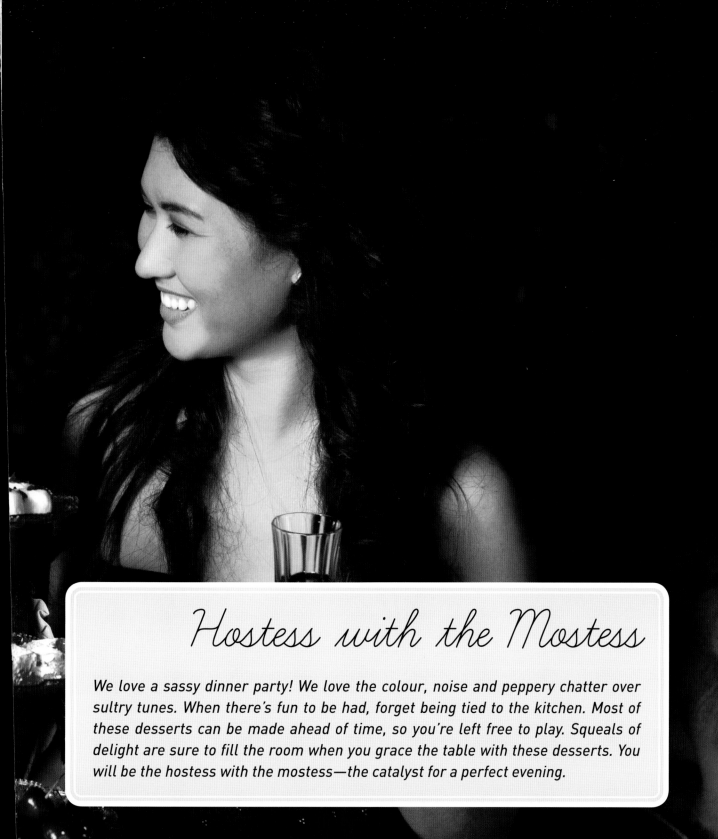

Hostess with the Mostess

We love a sassy dinner party! We love the colour, noise and peppery chatter over sultry tunes. When there's fun to be had, forget being tied to the kitchen. Most of these desserts can be made ahead of time, so you're left free to play. Squeals of delight are sure to fill the room when you grace the table with these desserts. You will be the hostess with the mostess—the catalyst for a perfect evening.

Turkish Oranges

Serves 4

Preparation time: 15 minutes

A popular Middle Eastern Dessert. Refreshing, light and bursting with goodness. The recipe is versatile too—the first time serve it as it appears below, then revisit it and try slicing the oranges then add to fruit salads, decorate a pavlova, or perhaps use as an addition to a punch or champagne cocktail...

4 large and firm oranges

200g (7oz) raw sugar

4 cloves

4 x 15ml (2fl oz) Cointreau or orange liqueur

Pure cream or Crème Fraîche Ice Cream, for serving

4 edible flowers for garnish

Pare the rind off the oranges with a knife leaving no pith behind. Take rinds and shred into fine strands and place in a bowl of boiling water for 5 minutes. Drain off the water, rinse and lay rind on paper towels to dry.

In a medium saucepan, place sugar, cloves and 350ml (11½oz) water on a medium heat, stirring until the sugar dissolves. Bring to the boil and leave without stirring, until a nice golden colour.

Place the peeled oranges in a baking dish along with shredded rind. Remove sugar syrup from the stove-top and carefully add the cointreau to syrup. Stir and pour over the oranges. Leave the oranges for 3 hours.

Occasionally, turn the oranges and the rind in the syrup.

Take one orange at a time and cut horizontally with a sharp knife. Be careful—use a fork to keep in place while doing so. Then rearrange as a whole orange on chosen dish and repeat. When four oranges are plated, spoon syrup over each orange, top with equal amounts of rind and garnish.

Serve with pure cream or Crème Fraîche Ice Cream (see Index).

Garnish each orange with an edible flower.

Hot Chocolate Vodka Shots

Makes 300ml (10½fl oz)

Serves 8–10 (shot glasses)

Chocolate Vodka is not for the faint hearted.

Note: *Add 10ml (1 tablespoon) Frangelico hazelnut liqueur for a Hazelnut Chocolate Vodka shot.*

200g (7oz) good-quality dark (semisweet), 70 or 85% cocoa, chocolate

150ml (5fl oz) vodka

Place vodka in a glass jar.

Fill a saucepan with boiling water, as deep as the level of vodka in the bottle/jar.

On a low heat, while attentively watching, immerse the jar in the water for a few minutes just to warm the vodka.

Chop the chocolate well, add to the jar , adding gradually and stirring until the warm vodka dissolves the chocolate and it appears the vodka cannot absorb the chocolate anymore. Remove from heat.

It is best to leave for at least 2 weeks in a dark cupboard.

When ready, serve warm in your desired shot glasses.

Chilli Chocolate Mousse

Serves 6
Preparation time: 30 minutes
Cooking time: 15 minutes

Who doesn't love chocolate? Like most, I have had a long-term love affair with Mr Chocolate. I have found that he loves all things spicy and I have given this mousse the ole Mayan spin by adding chilli. My favourite additions to this mousse are my Spicy Cherries (see Index) and fresh strawberries.

100g (3½oz) dark (semi-sweet), 70% cocoa, chocolate
100ml (3¼fl oz) milk
300ml 10fl oz) pouring cream
20g (⅔ oz) glucose syrup

¼ teaspoon chilli powder or ½ birdseye chilli, seeds in (leave out if you don't like chilli)
60g (2oz) caster (superfine) sugar
3 egg yolks

Prepare an ice-water bath by filling up a large bowl with ice and water and have a stainless-steel bowl with a fine sieve ready.

Place the chocolate in food processor or chop up into small pieces.

Over a very lightly simmering saucepan, place a heatproof bowl and melt your chocolate. Remove bowl from saucepan as soon as chocolate is melted. Keep warm.

In a saucepan, bring the milk, cream, glucose syrup, chilli and half of the caster sugar to just below boiling. In another bowl, beat the egg and half of the caster sugar until it is pale.

Gradually pour the hot cream mixture over the egg mix, whisking to combine, then pour this back into the saucepan. Stir continuously with a wooden spoon over a low heat until the mixture thickens enough to coat the back of a wooden spoon (about 84°C/185°F on a digital thermometer).

Whisk the custard slowly into the melted chocolate. Strain through a fine sieve into a bowl sitting in the larger bowl of ice. Stir to cool and then pour into beautiful glasses and pop in the fridge to set.

Garnish with fresh raspberries, strawberries, Spiced Cherries, Cardamom Oranges, Praline, a quenelle of Crème Fraîche Ice Cream or Tuiles (see Index).

Spiced Cherries

Preparation time: 15 minutes
Cooking time: 20 minutes

These spiced cherries speak of mulled wine, toasty Christmas moments around the fire, yet they somehow work in hot summer too. They are all spiced up, ready for action and make a juicy partner to my Chilli Chocolate Mousse or the Bittersweet Tarts (see Index).

½ cup light red wine (such as pinot noir)

35g (1¼oz) caster (superfine) sugar

1 orange, thinly sliced

½ lemon, juiced

1 cinnamon stick, lightly crushed

2 cloves (or 6 cardamom pods, crushed)

Pinch of nutmeg

¾ cup fresh cherries, pitted

Place the wine, sugar, orange slices, lemon juice, cinnamon, cloves (or cardamom) and nutmeg in a medium saucepan over low heat. Simmer, stirring occasionally, for 15 minutes.

Strain wine syrup and return to saucepan to simmer for another 10 minutes or until syrup starts to thicken.

Add cherries and simmer for 3–5 minutes stirring occasionally. Set aside to cool and infuse. You can reheat after at least half an hour to serve.

Champagne Sorbet

Serves 8

Preparation/Cooking time: 20 minutes

A recipe that is sure to impress anyone and is a great celebratory dessert. It is luxurious, elegant and somewhat indulgent. For best results, make this sorbet in an ice cream machine for a smooth and silky result. No Champagne? Try with sparkling wine or your other favourite wine.

300g (10½oz) caster (superfine) sugar

Juice of a grapefruit or lemon

2 tablespoons light corn syrup or liquid glucose

500ml (16fl oz) champagne

Place the sugar, 400ml (14fl oz) water, juice and corn syrup into a medium saucepan. Stir until all the sugar dissolves.

Increase heat and bring mixture to a rapid boil, then remove from heat and allow to cool to room temperature.

When completely cooled add the champagne.

Place into an ice cream machine. Follow the manufacturer's guidelines here. Generally, this will take about 30 minutes.

As it is delicate in nature, serve in delicate and elegant glassware, champagne flute or lovely glass bowls. Enjoy!

Cinnamon Chocolate Soufflé

Serves 4

Preparation time: 20 minutes

Cooking time: 10 minutes

Many people seem to be confronted by soufflé. It has such a sophisticated sounding name when really it is quite simple to make. Just make sure you serve your soufflé the minute it comes out of the oven. This is one of the easiest soufflé recipes you will find and you really will feel like a fancy-pants when you serve it to your guests.

I like a soufflé that is full-bodied and rich yet still lovely and light and this one is an absolute cracker.

Note: *Make a Simple Chocolate Ganache (see Index) and place some in the bottom of your soufflé for the most indulgent of indulgent soufflés.*

120g (4¼oz) dark (semisweet), 70% cocoa, chocolate

4 egg yolks (large eggs)

2 teaspoons ground cinnamon

8 egg whites (large eggs)

45g (1½oz) caster (superfine) sugar

Icing (confectioners') sugar, for dusting

Extra ground cinnamon, for dusting

Preheat oven to 190°C (375°F). Grab four soufflé dishes and grease with butter, coat with sugar and place on a baking tray.

Place the chocolate in food processor or chop up into small pieces.

Melt chocolate in a bowl over a saucepan of lightly simmering water, then whisk in egg yolks and cinnamon.

Beat the egg whites until soft peaks form, lightly pour sugar in and beat till stiff peaks form. Carefully whisk ¼ of the egg whites into the chocolate mixture. Then fold the rest of the egg whites in making sure that you don't knock all of the air out of the egg whites, by folding carefully.

Pour the mixture into the prepared soufflé dishes, filling almost to the top. Be sure to wipe the rims clean and lightly tap on bench to remove any big air bubbles. Place straight into the oven for 10 minutes or until the soufflé has risen nice and high. Dust with icing sugar and extra cinnamon and serve with a Crème Anglaise or whipped cream of choice (see Index).

Bay Pannacotta and Peaches

Serves 6

Preparation/Cooking time: 40 minutes

Refrigeration time: 7 hours

Things just seem to work when Lyndel and I put our heads together. The lovely Lyndel created this gorgeous Bay Pannacotta. It is truly one of my favourite recipes in this book. The perfect consistency, creamy with a slight tang, rounded off by the honey, makes it my favourite pannacotta recipe. The addition of the bay leaves and black pepper sits beautifully with my peach jelly. Feel free to try the other options of my tangy blood orange jelly or fig jelly. The fig jelly is truly a match made in heaven, with its sweet earthy tones.

Note: *If you are using a bigger jelly mould, you may want to set your jelly to one-third of your mould, place your fruit in and move to the fridge to set for 20 minutes. Then place more fruit and pour more jelly mixture on top. This will ensure that you get an even distribution of fruit and it won't all sink to the bottom.*

PEACH JELLY

2 gelatine leaves

300g (10½oz) caster (superfine) sugar

6 white peaches

Handful of seedless red grapes

Handful of raspberries

1½ tablespoons lemon juice

10 gold leaf gelatin leaves

PANNACOTTA

300ml (1¼ cups/10¼fl oz) cream

260g (9oz) unsweetened, plain yoghurt

3 gelatine leaves or 1¾ tablespoons powder

3½ tablespoons (40ml /1½oz) local honey

1 teaspoon vanilla paste

½ teaspoon black pepper

5 large bay leaves

PEACH JELLY

Grab two gelatine leaves and soften in a bowl of cold water for 5 minutes. Place 2L (70fl oz) water, lemon

Continues...

juice and sugar in a large saucepan and bring to the boil. Cover with a cartouche (see Glossary). Cut each of your lovely peaches into two cheeks.

Reduce the heat to low and place peach cheeks in the sugar syrup. Simmer gently for approximately 5 minutes. Remove from heat and leave the peaches in the syrup for another 5 minutes or until just slightly soft.

Measure out 1L (32fl oz) of the hot peach syrup. Squeeze out excess water from the gelatine leaves, add to the measured out syrup, stirring until the gelatine has dissolved. Pour jelly mixture into whatever size or shape ramekin ou desire, leaving plenty of room for a layer of pannacotta. Place a couple of your peach cheeks, raspberries and red grapes in your moulds, Place in your refrigerator to set for 30 minutes.

BAY PANNACOTTA

In a large bowl, whisk cream and yoghurt together, then set aside. Place gelatine leaves in cold water and set aside.

In a small saucepan, add 3½ tablespoons honey, vanilla, pepper and your bay leaves. On a low heat, bring the honey mixture to a simmer. Meanwhile remove excess liquid from the gelatine leaves, then add to the honey mixture, stirring until the gelatine has dissolved.

Remove from heat and whisk honey mixture (bay leaves and all) into the yoghurt mixture. Combine well, then strain mixture through a fine sieve into a jug for pouring. Pour on top of jelly and refrigerate until set. This will take about 7 hours or overnight if preferred.

TO SERVE

Dip the ramekins, one at a time, into a bowl of hot water for about 5 seconds. Run a knife around the edges of the ramekin bowl and carefully invert the pannacottas onto your desired chilled dessert plates. Your dinner guests are sure to be tickled pink with this stunning treat.

Blood Orange Jelly

Rather than using the peach jelly recipe, feel free to try these ones instead.

400ml (14fl oz) blood orange juice (approximately 8 oranges, if you can't find blood oranges you can use regular oranges)

4 gold leaf gelatine leaves

2 tablespoons honey

Grab the gelatine leaves and soften in a bowl of cold water for 5 minutes. Place the blood orange juice and honey in a saucepan over medium heat and remove just before it comes to the boil.

Squeeze out excess water from the gelatine leaves, add to the hot blood orange juice, stirring until the gelatine has dissolved. Pour jelly mixture into four 150ml (5fl oz) ramekins (whatever size or shape you desire really). Place in your refrigerator to set for 30 minutes.

Vanilla Bean Fig Jelly

400ml (14oz) syrup from Vanilla Bean Figs (see Index)

4 gold leaf gelatine leaves

2 tablespoons honey

Make the jelly exactly the same way as the blood orange jelly, but replace the blood orange juice with with 400ml of the syrup from the Vanilla Bean Figs.

Mulled Wine

Serves 12

Here is a mulled wine stunner. Great for parties all year round, but is especially delightful at Christmas no matter where you live. It is Christmas in a bottle. Keep it on the stove on a low heat just enough to keep the brew warm and serve to guests as they arrive. The aromas will fill the air and create a beautiful warm welcome. You and your guests will soon be feeling warm and fuzzy inside!

2 oranges

1 lemon

1 cup (225g/8oz) caster (superfine) sugar

5 cloves

1 whole nutmeg

1 vanilla pod, halved

1 cinnamon stick

3 fresh bay leaves

150ml (5fl oz) ginger wine

2 bottles of Chianti or other red wine

2 star anise

With a vegetable peeler remove the peel off the oranges and lemons, and then juice the fruit. Place peel and fruit into a large heavy based saucepan. Add the sugar, cloves, nutmeg (about 10 grates into the mix), vanilla pod, cinnamon stick, bay leaves and ginger wine.

Place on a low heat until the sugar dissolves. Then bring this mix to a rapid boil for 5 minutes or until a thick syrup develops.

Now, turn the heat to low and add your wine and the star anise. Stir to blend. Simmer on a low heat for 3 minutes (the more you simmer the more alcohol you remove from the brew).

Serve warm immediately, or bottle into sterilised jars for later and refrigerate.

Petit Fours

Chocolate Truffles

Makes about 25

Preparation time: 40 minutes

Cooking time: 20 minutes

A special treat fit to share with your closest friends, family or partner. They are so simple to make. Let your imagination run wild with different flavour combinations.

180ml (6fl oz) cream

140g (5oz) dark (semi-sweet), 70% cocoa, chocolate

80g (3 ½ oz) milk chocolate

30g (1oz) unsalted butter, cubed

50g (1 ¾ oz) cocoa

Place the cream in a saucepan on a medium heat and infuse with a flavour (options below). Bring cream to the boil. Remove from heat as soon as you see it start to boil and allow flavours to infuse for 30 minutes.

Place chocolate in a food processor or chop until you have tiny pieces of chocolate. Reheat cream so that it is just boiling again and then strain over chocolate and butter in a bowl, stirring until smooth and glossy. Cover with plastic wrap or pour into airtight container and refrigerate overnight.

Using a melon baller or teaspoon, create balls, roll in the cocoa and roll the balls in the palm of your hand. Refrigerate in an airtight container until ready to devour.

Flavours

Cardamom: Infuse cream with 1 teaspoon of crushed cardamom pods or ¾ teaspoon powdered cardamom.

Chilli: Chop up ½ red birds eye chilli, seeds included and infuse cream.

Coffee: Infuse cream with 2 ½ teaspoons of instant coffee.

Lavender: Infuse cream with a handful of dried lavender.

Lemongrass: Throw in 2 tablespoons of chopped lemongrass.

Mint: Infuse cream with a large handful of peppermint leaves or four peppermint tea bags.

Orange and Cardamom: Infuse cream with orange zest and add 10 crushed cardamom pods

White Chocolate and Cranberry Truffles

Makes about 25
Preparation time: 40 minutes
Cooking time: 20 minutes

You can use these little balls of goodness to coerce anyone into doing almost anything. Made for each other, white chocolate and cranberries are an unstoppable match.

220g (8oz) white chocolate
⅓ cup cream

Handful of cranberries (or hibiscus flowers, if available to you)

Place white chocolate in a food processor and process until you have tiny pieces of chocolate or cut up into small pieces with a knife.

Place the cream in a saucepan on a medium heat. Remove from heat as soon as you see it start to boil. Pour over chocolate in a bowl, stirring until smooth and glossy. Mix in your cranberries and cover with plastic wrap or pour into airtight container and refrigerate overnight.

Using a melon baller or teaspoon, create truffle balls and make them round by rolling in the palm of your hand. Keep them in an airtight container in the fridge or share them around for immediate gratification.

Turkish Delight

Makes 12 cubes

Preparation/Cooking time: 30 minutes

I delight in Turkish Delight! This is such a pleasure to make and share. Nothing beats fresh Turkish delight, it just melts in your mouth. Here is another recipe that you can play with. You can add nuts like almonds or pistachios, or even dried fruit like cranberries. I love it plain.

120g (4oz) cornflour

½ cup (125ml/4fl oz) warm water

½ cup (125ml/4fl oz) cold water

½ cup (125ml/4fl oz) orange juice (about the juice of 2 navel oranges)

1⅔ cups (375g/13oz) caster (superfine) sugar

1 teaspoon cream of tartar

2–3 drops of rosewater essence

2–3 drops natural red food colouring

Icing (confectioners') sugar or cornflour (cornstarch) to coat

Oil a small, glass baking dish (at times, I have even used shallow rectangular takeaway containers for this).

Stir the cornflour into the warm water, gradually. Mix, to remove all lumps and set aside.

In a small saucepan, mix water and juice, heat and then add the sugar. When mix reaches boiling point, reduce heat to low and add the cornflour mixture and the cream of tartar. Stir constantly while simmering for about 15 minutes.

Remove from heat and add flavouring and food colouring, if desired, and any nuts or fruit if you want.

Pour mixture into the prepared dish and chill in the fridge overnight to set. When cooled, cut jelly into squares. For best results, dip a sharp knife in hot water and this will make the cutting much easier.

Roll squares of jelly in icing sugar and cornflour mix (roughly equal portions), and store in an airtight container, place greaseproof paper between layers and extra dusting of sugar to prevent sticking.

This also makes a great gift.

Chocolate Cherries

Serves 8

Preparation time: 15 minutes

Cooking time: 10 minutes

Seductive, decadent and oh so so tasty. My chocolate cherries are perfect served as a petit four, at Christmas time as a sweet or hand-fed to your partner as the ultimate treat. For the cheekiest petit four, be sure to buy the freshest cherries from your local greengrocer.

500g (17½oz) fresh cherries

1 quantity of Simple Chocolate Ganache (Add 50g of extra chocolate. See Index, but use all dark chocolate for this recipe.)

Let your chocolate ganache cool slightly and then pour into a piping bag.

Take the pits out of your cherries using a cherry pitter or a small sharp knife. Try to keep the stalks in by putting the pitter right next to the stalk. If you lose a few stalks, no problem, you might have to fill them with chocolate and consume them immediately (purely for sustenance, of course).

Pipe the chocolate into the cherries, placing them bottom up on a plate and then pop them into the fridge to set for at least half an hour.

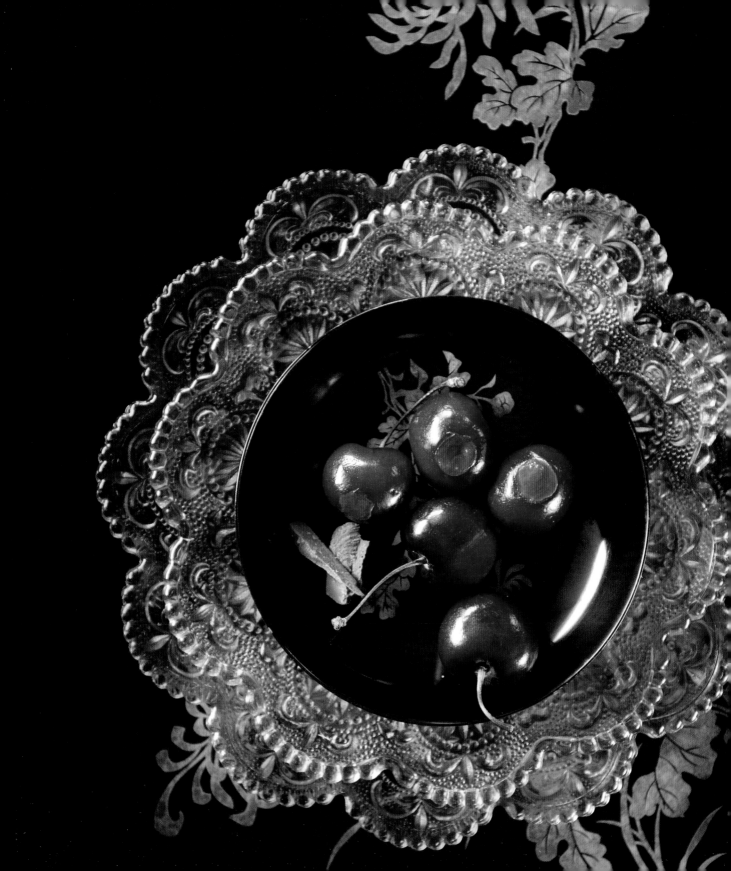

Bling

Dessert bling—snazzy little bits and pieces to accessorise your sweets. With a little imagination and this fine box of bling, you can make your desserts sparkle. And hey, there's nothing more fun than playing dress-ups.

Glass Ball (Spun Sugar)

Makes approximately 6 balls

The second time I ever made this delightful adornment was in the MasterChef kitchen. I proceeded to flip a tray of hot toffee upside down and producers are looking at me wondering what on earth I'm up to. I have my fingers crossed that it is going to work. Toffee strands began to set mid-air and collect onto a tray on the floor.
A gorgeous intricate ball of toffee begins to form and I breathe a huge sigh of relief.
It feels like magic every time you make these beautiful glass balls.

200g (7oz) caster (superfine) sugar
200g (7oz) or 200ml (7oz) glucose syrup

50g (1¾ oz) water

Combine all ingredients in a small saucepan. Stir over a low-medium heat. Once sugar has melted, increase heat to high. Cook for 15 minutes, until toffee is a very light golden colour or it registers 150°C (300°F) on a digital thermometer.

Line two baking trays with baking paper. I often use sticky tape to hold the paper onto the trays.

Pour the toffee onto one of the baking trays. Then put the empty baking tray on the floor. Wait approximately 30 seconds and test to see if the toffee is ready, by putting a fork into the toffee and pulling away. If the toffee strands start setting, it is ready for action! Turn the baking tray with the toffee upside down directly over the tray on the kitchen floor. Sugar strands will begin to set mid air. They will look like long strands of thin toffee—brittle but slightly bendy. Keep the toffee strands going toward the tray on the floor until there is no more toffee coming off the tray.

Quickly gather up the toffee strands and gently shape into small balls or whatever size you like. If you are not using immediately, put into a dry airtight container until ready to use these fascinating head turners.

You can reheat the unused toffee over a low heat, stirring constantly, and then create more balls the same way.

Continues...

Flavours

The glass balls are fabuloso as is. If you are up for a flavour adventure, then have fun with these yummy options, which are adjustable with just a few drops of this or that. When it comes to flavour choice, remember to be bold and brave. An extra large lemon glass ball or eucalyptus glass ball to accompany Karla's Citrus Tart (see Index) would be a dinner party jaw dropper.

Lemon: Add 3 drops of lemon juice (or lemon myrtle oil) to the toffee mixture when heating up.
Rose water: Add ¼ teaspoon rose water to the toffee mixture when heating up.
Eucalyptus: Add 3 drops eucalyptus oil to the toffee mixture when heating up. Eucalyptus oil taken in large
    quantities is toxic.
Vanilla: Add ¼ teaspoon vanilla essence to the toffee mixture when heating up.

GARNISH
Add a couple of edible flowers on each dessert. If that's too hard, don't worry about the garnish, the glass balls are exquisite as a garnish on their own.

Cardamom-spiced Oranges

Okay I'll admit it, I am an orange and cardamom fiend. In both sweet and savoury dishes, I keep being seduced by this utterly delightful partnership.

5 cardamom pods

4 oranges

1 tablespoon brown sugar

Pound the cardamom pods in a mortar and pestle, remove husks and grind cardamom seeds to a fine powder.

Juice one of the oranges and place the juice in a small bowl. Add the cardamom and sugar and stir until the mix has turned into syrup.

Using a sharp knife, peel the remaining three oranges, removing all pith. Slice into wedges by slicing in between the orange segments.

Place in bowl with juice and spice and throw in your fridge to macerate for 20 minutes.

Serve as an incredibly simple yet delicious accompaniment with Cinnamon Ice Cream, Karla's Citrus Tart, Bittersweet Chocolate Tart or with the Tangelo and Orange Blossom Cashew Cream (see Index).

Candied Citrus

Want to jazz up a simple orange or chocolate cake? This is great.

1 orange

1 lemon

250g (9oz) caster (superfine) sugar

Cut oranges and lemons into 4mm (just under ¼ inch) slices. Place the sugar into a heavy-based saucepan with 100ml (2¾fl oz) filtered water. Stir over a low heat until the sugar has completely dissolved. Bring to boil, then reduce heat and simmer for 10 minutes. Add the fruit slices and simmer a further 10–15 minutes, until translucent. Remove from stove then with tongs. Lift out the fruit and cool on a wire rack.

If you prefer to have thin strips of citrus, just remove peel from citrus and finely slice and add to pot.

Limoncello Glaze

Preparation time: 5 minutes

Limoncello was kindly introduced to me by an Italian friend of mine—Rob and his beautiful wife Louise. Limoncello is an Italian liqueur made from fermented lemons. Refreshing and light and always served as a cold beverage at the end of a meal, it is considered a digestive. The best limoncello comes from the Island of Capri and the Amalfi Coast. You can substitute Mandarinello (from mandarins) or Arancello (from oranges). And since you are buying a bottle, try limoncello with mineral water or champagne. I will be having it for summer with a serving of Blackberry, Elderberry and Lemon Mousse Trifle (see Index). This glaze is lovely over your chosen muffins, cakes, puddings or even over a scoop of ice cream.

190g (6¼oz) icing (confectioners') sugar
2 teaspoons fresh lemon juice

40ml (1½fl oz) limoncello

Simply whisk together and coat as desired.

Praline

Praline, with its shiny transparency, is the ultimate 'bling'. It is magnificent crushed into different consistencies, used to top icing on a cake, as an interesting addition to cookies, with ice cream and especially nice if you add this to ice cream and place this mix inside a bombe mould. Some like their praline to be loaded with nuts and, if you prefer it this way, just double the nut quantity in this recipe. You can also make it into Hazelnut Praline Butter (see Index).

½ cup (125g/4oz) hazelnuts, pistachios or
    macadamias, etc, roasted and unsalted
½ cup (115g/3¾oz) caster (superfine) sugar

80ml (2½fl oz) water
2 teaspoons malt vinegar

Prepare a baking tray with greaseproof paper and set aside.

In a small saucepan, on low heat, combine all ingredients, stirring once or twice, then wait until all the sugar dissolves. Increase heat and bring to a boil. Reduce heat, simmer uncovered without stirring for about 10 minutes or until syrupy and golden brown. Be attentive! The longer you cook the toffee the darker and harder it will set. If you are into gadgets and love the precision of a candy thermometer, a 'hard crack' is achieved between 138° and 154°C (280–310°F).

If you don't have one, like me, you can drizzle some of the hot toffee mixture into a bowl of cold water.

If it sets immediately and you can crack between your fingers, it is ready, if not cook a little longer.

Before you test this way, remove the pan from the heat and just wait a minute for the bubbles to subside. Add nuts. Pour mixture onto baking tray. Cool for about 15 minutes or until set. Should be hard and brittle. Break into preferred sizes or process, for a praline crumble.

Hazelnut Praline Butter

Preparation/Cooking time: 15 minutes

In France, jars of praline paste or what I like to call praline butter, can be found on café tables for all to share. You have to try this! Leave guilt at bay and allow yourself to enjoy this taste sensation. This paste resembles peanut butter and is deliciously creamy—sweet with a hint of crunch. Enjoy on toast, in porridge, as a topping on ice cream, mixed in cream cheese for a yummy icing on a coffee or chocolate cake (and sprinkle some crushed praline for added sparkle) or if you are 'off the wagon', eat it by the spoonful.

1 cup (250g/9oz) hazelnut praline (see recipe for Praline in Index)

1 cup (250g/9oz) hazelnuts, roasted, skins removed

80ml (2½fl oz) hazelnut oil, to taste (if you cannot find hazelnut oil just use any neutral vegetable oil)

Pinch of salt

Break prepared praline up into small enough pieces for your processor to handle.

To a food processor, add the praline, nuts, oil and salt. Pulse until you reach your desired consistency then dig in!

Frosts

For icing, filling cakes and cupcakes, these frosts are sensational with flavours to inspire you to create magnificence.

Piccolo

250g (8oz) unsalted butter

250g (8oz) cream cheese

200g (6½oz) icing (confectioners') sugar

30ml (1fl oz) espresso or prepared instant coffee

Combine all the ingredients in a mixing bowl and mix until smooth and creamy. And if you are a coffee fiend, you might want to add extra strong brew here!

Peanut Frosting

250g (8 oz) unsalted butter

250g (8 oz) cream cheese

200g (6 ½ oz) icing (confectioners') sugar

150g (4 ¾ oz) peanut butter (or other nut butter of choice)

Combine all ingredients in a mixer bowl, and mix until smooth and creamy.

    Remember: Most schools these days ban peanut products, so don't make the mistake of using this icing for a school fete or child's lunchbox.

Cream Cheese Frosting

250g (9oz) unsalted butter

250g (9oz) cream cheese

200g (7oz) icing (confectioners') sugar

1 teaspoon vanilla paste/extract

Combine all ingredients in a bowl and mix until smooth and creamy.

Ginger Frosting

100g (3½oz) unsalted butter

250g (9oz) cream cheese

300g (10½oz) icing (confectioners') sugar

125g (4oz) glacé ginger, finely chopped

Combine butter, cream cheese and icing sugar in a bowl and mix until smooth and creamy. Stir in the chopped ginger.

Black Cherry and Vanilla Frosting

100g (3½oz) unsalted butter

250g (9oz) cream cheese

300g (10½oz) icing (confectioners') sugar

50g (1¾oz) black cherries (about 8 cherries)

100g (3½oz) sour cream

½ teaspoon vanilla paste/extract

Combine all ingredients in a bowl and mix until smooth and creamy.

Coconut Frosting

100g (3½oz) unsalted butter

250g (9oz) cream cheese

300g (10½oz) icing (confectioners') sugar

80ml (2½fl oz) coconut milk

200g (7oz) desiccated coconut

Combine all ingredients (except desiccated coconut) in a bowl and mix until smooth and creamy, then fold in desiccated coconut.

Chocolate Frosting

100g (3½oz) unsalted butter

250g (9oz) cream cheese

300g (10½oz) icing (confectioners') sugar

100g (3½oz) cacao/cocoa powder

150g (5oz) sour cream

Combine all ingredients in a bowl and mix until smooth and creamy.

Citrus Frosting

100g (3½oz) unsalted butter

250g (9oz) cream cheese

300g (10½oz) icing (confectioners') sugar

80ml (2½fl oz) lemon, orange or mandarin juice

100g (3½oz) zest

Combine all ingredients in a bowl and mix until smooth and creamy.

Berry Frosting

100g (3½oz) unsalted butter

250g (9oz) cream cheese

300g (10½oz) icing (confectioners') sugar

50g (1¾oz) berries (of your choice) strained through a fine sieve to remove seeds

½ teaspoon vanilla extract

Combine all ingredients in a bowl and mix until smooth and creamy.

Maple Honey Frosting

250g (8oz) unsalted butter, softened

250g (8oz) cream cheese

200g (6½oz) icing (confectioners') sugar

⅓ cup (50g/1¾oz) brown sugar

¾ cup (180ml/6fl oz) maple syrup or local honey

Combine all the ingredients in a mixing bowl and mix until smooth and creamy.

Pine Frosting

100g (3½oz) unsalted butter

250g (9oz) cream cheese

300g (10½oz) icing (confectioners') sugar

50g (1¾oz) crushed pineapple

Combine all ingredients in a bowl and mix until combined and creamy.

Carrot Cake Frosting

Especially for a carrot cake, this is for a tiered cake that requires more icing and lashings of it.

50g (1¾oz) unsalted butter

300g (10½oz) icing (confectioners') sugar

350g (12oz) cream cheese

2 teaspoon lemon juice

Combine all ingredients in a mixer and mix until smooth and creamy.

Flavoured Creams

Chantilly Cream

1 cup (235g/8oz) pouring cream

2 tablespoons icing (confectioners') sugar, sifted

1 vanilla bean (cut down centre and scrape inside) or 1 teaspoon vanilla extract

Whip all ingredients together until soft peaks form.

Raspberry Cream

1 cup (190g/6½oz) fresh or frozen raspberries, thawed

1 cup (235g/8oz) pouring cream

3 tablespoons icing (confectioners') sugar, sifted

Puree raspberries in a blender, then strain through a fine sieve. Whip cream to soft peaks and then fold in raspberry puree.

You can play with other fruit such as strawberries, mangoes or apricots.

Cinnamon Cream

1 cup (235g/8oz) pouring cream

2 tablespoons icing (confectioners') sugar, sifted

1 teaspoon cinnamon

Combine all ingredients together and whip to firm peaks.

Chocolate Cream

1 cup (235g/8oz) pouring cream

2 tablespoons icing (confectioners') sugar, sifted

1 teaspoon cinnamon

Combine all ingredients together and whip to firm peaks.

Orange and Thyme Cream

1 cup (235g/8oz) pouring cream

2 tablespoons icing (confectioners') sugar

1 teaspoon orange zest, finely grated

1 tablespoon fresh squeezed orange juice

¼ teaspoon dried thyme

Combine all ingredients together and whip to firm peaks.

Rose Cream

1 cup (235g/8oz) pouring cream

2½ tablespoons icing (confectioners') sugar

¼ teaspoon rose water

Combine all ingredients together and whip to firm peaks. You can substitute the rose water for orange blossom water too.

Tuiles

Delicious and scrum-diddli-umptious! A great dessert garnish or accompaniment. They are perfect to add texture to anything light or delicate. I think they are perfect for any mousse.
This recipe is super easy to make and remember!

70g (2¼oz) plain (all-purpose) flour

100g (3½oz) caster (superfine) sugar

70g (2¼oz) unsalted butter, melted

100g (3½oz) egg white (3–4 eggs)

Pinch of salt

Addition butter for greasing

1 tablespoon sliced almonds, or spiced tuiles, add pepper or cinnamon to taste (optional)

Preheat oven 180°C (350°F/Gas Mark 4). Line 2 baking trays with greaseproof baking paper, and grease well with butter. Set aside.

In a medium bowl, combine the flour and sugar. Set aside. In another bowl, combine melted butter and egg whites and stir. Combine wet and dry ingredients and then place into a container and place in fridge for at least one hour.

Remove batter from fridge. Spread a thin layer of batter onto one prepared tray. Bake for 8 minutes.

Remove tuiles from oven and turn onto the other prepared tray. Cut the tuile into 5cm (1in) strips that run the length of tray. Return to oven and cook until golden brown.

Remove and, working quickly, twist the strips of tuile around a rolling pin one at a time, while still hot. This will create a curl. Allow the tuiles to cool completely before storing in an airtight container.

Sugared Rose Petals

These are a charming touch on a dessert, especially when you are preparing something special for someone you love. A lovely touch on Valentine's Day; serve as you please.

1 egg white

½ cup (110g /4oz) caster (superfine) sugar

15 unsprayed rose petals

In a small bowl, whisk the egg white well. Prepare two baking trays with baking paper and spread the sugar evenly over a dinner plate. Take the rose petals and brush beaten egg white on each petal. Drain on baking paper then place on the dinner plate with sugar and coat each petal well.

Place the sugar-covered petals gently onto the other prepared tray and then leave tray in a well-ventilated and cool, dry place for about 2 hours to dry completely.

Balsamic Berries

This makes a very simple, but enjoyable sweet. Balsamic with berries is an old Italian trick. The balsamic vinegar beautifully enhances the colour and taste of the berries that they befriend.
So easy to prepare and so versatile. Berries are great alone, with cream, ice cream or yoghurt,as a dressing for pavlova or with a simple pound cake.

30ml (1fl oz) balsamic vinegar

60g (2oz) caster (superfine) sugar

20ml (²/₃ fl oz) lemon juice

500g (17½ oz) berries of your choice, if you choose strawberries, and they are rather large, cut into halves or quarters

In a large saucepan, place vinegar, sugar and lemon juice. Then on a medium heat, simmer for 5 minutes until all the sugar dissolves. Remove from heat and cool.

Place berries in a large bowl, and when syrup has cooled pour over the fruit and toss well.

Cover with cling film and refrigerate for at least an hour.

Sweet Cinnamon Nuts

Preparation time: 10–15 minutes

Cooking time: 30 minutes

Spiced nuts are divine. Whip these up for guests to enjoy with a drink or as part of a party menu. You can play around with the choices of nuts and spices to suit your tastes, menu and guests. Once you make one batch you will be hooked!

Butter or ghee, for greasing

2 egg whites

Pinch of salt

80g (2½oz) caster (superfine) sugar

80g (2½oz) raw (Demerara) sugar

1 tablespoon cinnamon, ground

600g (1lb 5oz) nuts (macadamias, Brazil, almonds or hazelnuts)

3 tablespoons vanilla paste or extract

Preheat oven 160°C (325°F/Gas Mark 2 -3). Line a large roasting pan with greaseproof paper, and grease with butter or ghee.

Using an electric mixer, beat the eggs and salt until frothy. Add the caster sugar gradually, beating the mixture constantly, until all is well combined. Then gradually add the demerara sugar and cinnamon to the egg whites mixture until well combined.

Then take a medium mixing bowl, add nuts, vanilla, then egg mixture and combine well. I like to use my hands here so I get a nice and even distribution as all the nuts need to be well-coated. Spread onto the prepared tray or trays.

Bake for 30–35 minutes. Remove from oven and cool completely. Break into pieces if necessary and store in an airtight container. These should keep for 2 weeks.

About the Authors

Skye Craig

Skye has come a long way since she learnt to make pikelets as a seven-year-old from a cookbook that her mum gave her. Hailed for her unorthodox methods and decadent desserts on the second series of MasterChef, Skye Craig fast became known in lounge rooms as the dessert queen. Her years working as a graphic designer and her insatiable passion for desserts has propelled her into her new business Wild Sugar where she continues to inspire and delight with her unique and decadent sweets. Her desserts are a celebration of the naughty gene that lives within all of us. She is also passionate about finding ways to treat and nurture in ways that serve us well. From recipes made from healthy ingredients to gratifying chocolate-laden desserts, you'll find a sweet treat from *Wild Sugar Desserts* to put a smile on your face. Her desserts are a treasure trove of pleasures, so dig in and enjoy. Life is a wild ride. Sweets remind us to smile. www.wildsugar.com.au

Lyndel Miller

A mother of two with an all-consuming affection for entertaining in all its delicate and delicious detail, Lyndel Miller is living the life of her dreams as a food, prop and interior stylist. She marvelled at the effects her mother's cooking would have on her devoted public and how it would act as a profound catalyst to bring people together and celebrate. Now, Lyndel has successfully intertwined the two into her short but stellar career. Starved for creativity, Lyndel set aside her fledging naturopathy career to embrace studies in interior design and colour. Sophisticated, emotive and original, Lyndel's talents were quickly recognised by Skye Craig, with whom Lyndel has joyously styled this book. *Wild Sugar Desserts* is Lyndel's first cookbook and is the total embodiment of her spirit and style. Lyndel creates a welcome in her home, where you will find love in every gesture. There is always a chair open at her table.

Handy Tips

Baking powder is two parts cream of tartar, and one part bicarbonate of soda (baking soda).

Raw caster (superfine) sugar is known as golden caster sugar in the UK. It offers the subtle presence of molasses and is a less processed choice.

Roll tins When roll tins are unavailable, be thrifty and make your own tin rolls for baking by using tall 850ml (8 x 17cm or 3 x 6in) fruit juice cans. Remove lid and bottom of can with a can opener that cuts just below the rim. Wash and dry cans well before you grease them.

Sweet shortcrust pastry can be made in a food processor as long as you are fast on the 'pulse' button, so as not to overwork the pastry.

To get more juice out of your citrus you can roll the fruit back and forth on a flat surface, pressing fruit, or place your fruit in a microwave for 10 seconds on High at 100 per cent before squeezing them.

To use a vanilla bean pod, cut the bean in half lengthways and then scrape out the seeds and the pulp. In some recipes you can then add all to the mix and then remove the pod after cooking. You can also wash the vanilla bean and dry thoroughly, then add to your caster sugar to have vanilla-flavoured sugar on hand in the pantry.

Measuring cups The difference between an American and an Australian measuring cup is so small that most just don't worry. But it is important to note that the Australian tablespoon is different to the rest of the world.

Ovens When baking be mindful that your oven is different to my oven and your neighbour's oven. Always check on your baking. If a skewer comes out clean, it's ready.

Edible flowers All flowers must be home-grown to be consumed. You may be able to find these at specialty local greengrocers or grow your own. Examples are orange blossom, lilac, borage, violet, elderberry and English primrose.

1 Australian cup is 250ml / American 237ml
1 Australian tablespoon is 20g / American 15g

To soften cream cheese easily, place portion in a zip lock plastic bag and place in hot water for a few minutes. The colder the cream the faster it whips.

If you need to check the freshness of an egg, float it in a bowl (in its shell) in a large bowl of room-temperature water. The older the egg, the high it floats. (If it just breaks the water surface, it won't be great for poaching).

If you use a spritzer when spraying warm ghee (in case of baklava) or melted butter, you will use less and the result will be lighter and contain less fat.

For ease of cutting a cake for a dinner party into small portions, put a cylinder in the middle of the cake, (use a saucer, pot lid or nut roll tin) and then cut the outer ring into wedges. When the outside of the cake is gone, you are left with a small round cake for another time.

To make a quenelle, place a spoon in hot water and then drag the spoon through your cream, ice cream or sorbet until it curls over and forms a round quenelle. Place on your desired dessert for pure chefy goodness.

Glossary

Agave nectar, honey or maple syrup can be bought from a health food store. If using honey, try to buy raw honey if you can, as it hasn't been heat-treated and still contains all of the wonderful nutritional content.

Baking soda (bi-carb) is sodium bicarbonate, a leavening agent that causes batter to rise when baked. It has numerous uses outside of cooking too.

Bombe is a name for a frozen dessert consisting of layers of ice cream or sorbet that is placed in a round or cylindrical mold. A true bombe has an outer layer of ice cream and soft filling (usually not another ice cream).

Cartouche is a circle of baking paper that you place over a sauce or liquid you are cooking to stop a skin forming. Make the circle the same size as the inside of the pan you are using.

Cashews (raw and unsalted) are smooth, creamy coloured, kidney-shaped nuts. The hard shell of the cashew is actually toxic and this is why we only see them shelled.

Due to their high fat content they do turn rancid quickly, so store them in an airtight container or a plastic bag. You can freeze them for up to nine months in the freezer. They can be can be bought from a supermarket or a health food store.

Caster sugar is superfine granulated sugar.

Coconut oil The fatty oil obtained from the coconut. Stimulates thyroid function, anti-aging, weight loss stimulating and has wonderful antiseptic properties. It can be bought from a health food store. Unrefined coconut oil can have quite a strong flavour. If you don't want a coconut-flavoured dessert, use a refined coconut oil or 'coconut butter', as it provides the fat content without overpowering the other flavours in the dessert.

Cointreau or Triple Sec is a colourless orange flavoured liqueur.

Cream of tartar or tartaric acid is an acid used in baking. It is used to stabilise the whites of eggs and give them strength and volume. It is also used to prevent crystallization in sugar syrups. It is usually found in baking or spice sections of your supermarket.

Crème fraîche A thick cream made from heavy cream with the addition of buttermilk, sour cream or yoghurt. Slightly fermented and thickened with lactic acid. Sour in taste and originally from France. If unavailable, substitute with sour cream.

Demerara sugar is a light-brown cane sugar.

Digestive biscuit A sweet meal or semi sweet biscuit.

Elderflower cordial Elderflower has a distinctive floral fragrance. Elderflower comes traditionally from Europe.

Frosting Also known as icing. A name used to describe a sweet, sugary mix used to dress and fill layers of cakes.

Ganache A term used to describe a smooth silky mixture of chocolate and cream.

Gelatine is an odourless, tasteless and colourless thickening agent. Gelatine forms a semi-solid colloid gel. Melts to a liquid when heated and solidifies when cooled again to form jelly. Need to add more detail here

Ghee, also known as clarified butter or drawn butter, is simply unsalted butter that has had the milk solids and water removed, so it then becomes pure yellow butterfat. It can be substituted for butter in most recipes (but not the other way around).

Icing sugar (confectioners' sugar) A fine powdered sugar used to make icing.

Lemongrass A fragrant tropical grass that yields a lemony aroma. Native to Southern India and Sri Lanka, it is a natural remedy to promote clear skin and aid digestion too.

Liquid glucose A thick, sweet, clear syrup derived from many sources of starch. Some are wheat derived, some derived from corn starch, so if gluten intolerant check your labels. Liquid glucose is used to control the formation of sugar crystals. Used frequently in the making of ice creams and other frozen desserts.

Macadamia (raw and unsalted) A small, round, ivory-coloured nut meat that has a hard brown shell. It is prone to rancidity due to its high fat content so best stored in an airtight container. Can be stored in the freezer for up to a year.

Marsala is a sweet dessert wine produced in the region surrounding the Italian city of Marsala in Sicily.

Mascarpone is a soft, unripened cheese that belongs to the cream cheese family. I use whipped cream as a substitution usually. It comes from Switzerland.

Palm sugar Originally made from the sap of the date palm, but now is also made from the sap of sago, arenga, pinnata and coconut palms. Also known as arenga sugar or coconut sugar.

Parfait is generally a layered dessert containing fruits, creams and syrups. French for perfect.

Pecans A smooth nutshell that contains an ivory-coloured nut meat that is golden brown with wrinkled lobes. It is soft-textured, buttery, slightly bitter and is enhanced greatly when toasted. Over 70 per cent fat, so like most nuts they can turn rancid quickly. Keep them in an airtight container or plastic bag, either in the fridge for three months or up to six months in the freezer.

Ramekins A small dish for baking individual portions of food.

Raw cacao has sixteen times more anti-oxidants than red wine, it is a source of beta-carotene, amino acids (protein), Omega-3 EFA's, calcium, zinc, iron, copper, sulphur, potassium, and one of the best food sources of muscle relaxing, stress relieving magnesium. Will also keep you up all night if you eat too much too late in the day.

Raw cacao butter Pure stable fat that is pressed out of cacao beans. It has the beautiful rich aroma of dark chocolate.

Raw sugar A type of light brown coarse sugar still containing the natural molasses present in sugar cane.

Sago is an edible starch that is obtained from the pith of sago palm stems. It is native to high elevations in Asia.

Savoiardi biscuits are an Italian sponge biscuit, which you can buy from the supermarket.

Tangelos A hybrid of the tangerine and either the pomelo or the grapefruit. It tastes like a tangerine and has more juice than pulp.

Tuiles French for tile. So named, as tuiles resembled the shape of roof tiles in France. They are a very thin, crisp and brittle cookie, traditionally made with almonds.

Index

Credits

Thanks to:

Karen and Paul Craig, Simon Miller and Damon Hughes, thanks for everything! We are incredibly grateful. Greg Pead of Retrosheila, who lives and breathes vintage! The real deal. Designers: Lisa Brown, Emma Milikins, Karen Neilsen, Lazybones—thanks Nicole, Don't Tell Fanny—thanks Paige, House of Harlow. Prop Hire: Lyndel Miller, Rebecca Todd of Fancy Tea (phenomenal!), Judi and Kris of Little Gray Station, Olivia and Joanna of Grit and Glamour, Found Furniture—Matt Hatcher and Kelly Nuss and Georgia at Little Love and Happiness for flowers. Wardrobe/Styling Assistants: Kirsten Baker (really lovely work on kids' party clothing and talent—thank you), Holly Robinson, Ashleigh WIlliams and Alex Fitzgerald, Nicole Gibson.

Make-up assistants: Amanda Teasdale, Haley Hughes, Holly Hughes, Aleisha Gannon and Melissa Preston. Hair: Gastar Hair—Lauren Mitchel and many thanks to Gregson Gastar. Hair assistants: Dan Payne, Grace Hogan from Gastar Hair. Talent: Nicholas Morton, Julia Skalski, Andrew Cottle, Holly Robinson. Division Model Management: Christy, Angie and Tara. Kiddliwinks: Tahlia, Sam, Vivi, Alex, Thomas, Erin, Miranda (and their mums and dads). Academy of Design: Rycki Symons, Cindy Soulsby, Paul Phillips, Caio Ezto, Rhiannon Porter, Rachel Ogle. Catering: Marina Carta at Toolona Street Food Store and Erin Fayers. Beautiful fresh produce from Your Local Greengrocer (www.everybodysbody.com.au) (thanks to Rebecca Clingan for your assistance with produce) and Express Wholesalers. Victoria Fletcher, Beau and Jake Maynard, you all rock.

A special thank you to all our amazing recipe testers! We are most appreciative. Many gold stars and a scratch and sniff sticker to you: Adele Fragnito, Alisha May, Amanda Miller, Angela Twining, Annique Rousseau, Anthony Nelson, Ashleigh Mackney, Betty Craig AKA Nanna, Carole Seymour, Catherine Pepper, Chemai Mc Kendry, Christine Danielle Low, Claire Winton Burn, Cynthia Seguin, David Watts, Emma Miller, Gemma and Ellie—Maree Miskell, Gilda Cohen-Shapira, Hayley Riddle AKA The Scarlet Cob, Helen Langston, Jackie Rousseau (Canada), Janna Theunert (Germany), Jase Boyes AKA Sir Jason Boyes, Jesslee Engelhardt, Jonathan Russell AKA Rock Hardson, Karen Craig, Karla Novack, Kathleen Browne, Katie Miller, Katie Pepper, Kelli Betti, Kim Whiley, Kylie Craig, Kylie Mitchell–Smith, Martin Shang AKA The Shang, Meg Kelly, Meredith Myers, Cynthia and Caleb Séguin, Michelle Jessop AKA BBBBBF, Michelle Lewis, Michelle Spense AKA Muzzas, Moana and Aroha Peni (NZ), Natasha Conrad, Nikki Ellis, Paula Johnston, Phil Dudman, Rebecca Wintle, Rene Renee, Robyn Butel, Roy Schack, Sam Savara, Sam Yau, Sharan Kafoa, Stephan Conrad, Tracy Hopley, Tulsi Van De Graaff, Wendy Chapman. We hope we haven't missed anyone, sincere apologies if we have and many thanks for your kind help.

xxx Skye and Lyndel

First published in 2012 by
New Holland Publishers Pty Ltd
Sydney • Auckland • London • Cape Town

www.newhollandpublishers.com
www.newholland.com.au

Garfield House 86–88 Edgware Road London W2 2EA United Kingdom
1/66 Gibbes Street Chatswood NSW 2067 Australia
Wembly Square First Floor Solan Street Gardens Cape Town 8000 South Africa
218 Lake Road Northcote Auckland New Zealand

ISBN 9781742572154

Publisher: Lliane Clarke
Project Editor: Jodi De Vantier
Cover and Graphic Design: Celeste Vlok
Photography: Celeste Vlok and Mindi Cooke
Art Direction Photography: Skye Craig
Stylist, Food Stylist, Prop Stylist, Model Stylist: Lyndel Miller
Styling Assistant: Annique Rousseau
Food Styling Assistant: Julie Ray
Production Manager: Olga Dementiev
Printer: Toppan Leefung Printing
10 9 8 7 6 5 4 3 2 1

Follow New Holland Publishers on Facebook:
www.facebook.com/NewHollandPublishers